~ New

Fortified & Enlarged Edition

Forgiven Forever

The title is gleaned from the aorist Greek tense found in 1 John 1:9

The truth found in this book will set you free

Hector C. MacLeod

Author of

"Behold the Lamb"

Copyright © by Hector C. MacLeod 1997

Revised Edition – Second Printing – 2000

Canadian Cataloguing in Publication Data

MacLeod, Hector C. (Hector Charles) 1920–
Forgiven Forever

Includes bibliographical references and index
ISBN 0-920225-09-8

1. Forgiveness --Biblical teaching--Christianity.   I. Title
BS680.F64M32 1997   2345   C97-910707-5

Printed in Canada by
Quadra Printers Ltd., 2217 Wilgress Road, Nanaimo, British Columbia

TABLE OF CONTENTS

TABLE OF CONTENTS

PROLOGUE

When I began a research into the true meaning of 1John1:9 and to whom it applies, I never for a moment expected that it would be large enough to warrant a book-size publication. However, when I handed out the many pages of my research, first to close Christian friends and then on a somewhat wider scale, I saw that God's people were receiving the truths it contained and were being released in a wonderful way, as I had been released myself by the powerful message of the Word of God. When my eyes were opened to see that 1John1:9 was directed to **the sinner outside of Christ** and not directed to the believer who is totally forgiven, justified, and clothed with God's righteousness forever, I sensed a marvelous release that has never left me. **HIS BLESSED WORD ALWAYS DEMONSTRATES THE FINALITY OF HIS FORGIVENESS AT THE CROSS.** All those who believe are sealed with the Holy Spirit until the day of redemption. They are never told to confess their sins, but are assured again and again that Christ has entered *"into heaven itself, now to appear in the presence of God FOR US"* (Heb.9:24). *"We have an advocate with the Father, Jesus Christ the Righteous"* (1John 2:1).*"He ever liveth to make intercession for us"* (Heb.7:25).

Those who received the first papers of this

research urged me to have the work published. I have to be honest and admit that I was somewhat reluctant to go ahead with its publication because it is so contrary to the traditional notion that I myself taught for many years. However, our research in the blessed Word of God proved overwhelmingly that the traditional interpretation of 1John1:9 can never be reconciled with the other truths of the New Testament.The teaching on believers' confession of sin is so common and generally accepted that it is probable you never thought of testing it thoroughly with the Word of God. Please be aware as you read this book that we are doing just that.

The traditional interpretation of 1John1:6-9 found in most commentaries of the Bible is by and large the following:

Every time a believer sins he must confess that sin and ask God for forgiveness. It further teaches that when a believer sins he loses fellowship with God that cannot be restored until confession is made.

Carefully analyze the above interpretation and note how man has taken the driver's seat.

1. The confessor, if diligent and faithful, is restoring himself and needs to be credited for it.

2. The FINISHED work of our Lord on the Cross is largely ignored (John 19:30).

3. The gift of righteousness, once and for all given by God, is left entirely out of the picture (John 3:16; Romans 5:17; Ephesians 2:8,9).

4. God's act of justifying the believer, once and for all, the instant he believes, is totally robbed of its true meaning (Acts 13:35,39; Romans 4:5;8:30).

We hope that you too will see that the following truths from the eternal Word of God quickly show up the error of the above interpretation. They declare with positive language that the sinner is saved and totally forgiven for sins of the past, sins of the present and sins of the future the instant he trusts the Saviour.

1. Our Saviour *"put away sin by the sacrifice of Himself"* (Heb.9:26).

2. *"He saves them to the uttermost that come unto God by Him, seeing HE ever liveth to make intercession for them"* (Heb.7:25).

3. *"We are sanctified through the offering of the body of Jesus Christ once for all"* (Heb.10:10).

4. *"By one offering He hath perfected forever them that are sanctified" (Heb.10:14).* When we view the common interpretation of 1John 1:9 in the light of Scripture it is really a doctrine of works. It seems that man is determined to have a part somewhere in his own salvation. He is not

prepared to accept, without reservation, the finished work of our blessed Saviour on the Cross and *HIS* ongoing intercession on our behalf. The Word of God, however, distinctly declares that the believer is on the receiving end of everything. *"For who has first given to Him, and it shall be recompensed to Him again? For of Him, and through Him, and to Him, are all things: to whom be glory forever" (Romans 11:35,36).* All those who are believers, therefore, can only *"Offer the sacrifice of praise to God CONTINUALLY, that is, the fruit of our lips giving thanks to His name"* (Heb.13:15).

"Before you read further in this book, we want to make it crystal clear that we agree wholeheartedly with the true meaning of the word **confession**, and also with what the Spirit of God is teaching in 1 John 1:9. If we did not, you would be wise to relegate this book to the garbage bin where it would belong.

Every Bible student who has studied the original Greek of the New Testament has to agree that the word translated **confession** in 1 John 1:9 simply means **to say the same thing**. We are to agree with God that we are sinners. With reference to 1 John 1:9, Dr. J. Vernon McGee writes, *"What does it mean to confess our sins? Confess is from the Greek verb*

homologea *meaning* **to say the same thing.** *Logio means* **to say** *and* **homo** *means* **the same.** *You are to say the same thing God says".* 1. If we check all Greek and English dictionaries, we discover that they are in perfect accord with Dr. McGee's translation. When we understand exactly what our great God is teaching in 1 John 1:9, there is no possible way that we can extract from that verse the traditional notion that believers need to probe into their lives, trying to determine where and when they have sinned in order that they might spell it out to God, asking His forgiveness over and over again. The aforementioned fact ought to be repeated at least seven more times in order that it not be missed by anyone.

When we thoroughly research 1 John 1:9 two critical questions come to mind. 1. Who is John addressing? He cannot be addressing forgiven sinners. Why? Because forgiven sinners had to *(homologeo)* i.e. agree with God that they were sinners in order to be saved. 2. Furthermore, the tense used in that verse (in the original) indicates an on-going *(homologeo)*, i.e. a constant agreement with God that we are sinners. Believers who have received the Lord Jesus as their Saviour are the only ones on earth who totally fulfill 1 John 1:9. All true believers are ever in agreement with God that they are sinners and are in continual need of Jesus Christ our Saviour *"whoever liveth to make intercession for us"* (Heb. 7:25).

Since John evidently was not addressing believers, who then was he targeting in 1 John 1:9? Were there people at the time of John's writing who refused to agree with God that they were sinners? Yes indeed there were. They were known as Gnostics. They mingled themselves among true believers in the early Church. They taught that the soul and spirit of man was untainted by sin, only the body and all matter was evil. The International Standard Bible Encyclopaedia states: *"In the First Epistle of John there is a distinct polemical purpose. There is no book in the N.T. which is more purposeful in its attack of error ... This peril, against which the apostle writes, and from which he seeks to defend the Church, was Gnosticism, as is proved by what is said again and again in the epistle of the characteristics of this insidious and deadly teaching"*. 2. (See chapter 5 for more on Gnostic heresy).

If born again believers never committed sins, our Lord's present office as intercessor would be totally unnecessary. The instant we receive Christ, He enters in to take up residence with the promise that He will remain with us forever. When He initially enters in, we often see ourselves as we have never seen ourselves before: sinful, vile, and in desperate need of an advocate. As a result of this many new believers doubt the reality of their salvation.

Every believer who is truly born of God's Spirit can ever chorus with the apostle Paul who declared: ***"For I know that in me, [that is, in my flesh] dwelleth no good thing; for to will is present with me, but how to perform that which is good I find not"*** (Romans 7:18*). "This is a faithful saying, and worthy of all acceptance, that Christ Jesus came into the world to save sinners, of whom I am chief"* (1 Tim. 1:15). The words of the apostle recorded in Timothy were spoken near the end of his life on earth. The apostle Paul was always aware that he was a sinner. The Spirit of God is ever faithful to remind all of us of the fact. Paul therefore, always lived in fulfillment of 1 John 1:9 which clearly states, in the original, "If we go on agreeing with God *(homologeo)* that we are sinners, He is faithful and just to [have] (aorist tense) forgiven us our sins, and to [have] (aorist tense) cleansed us from all unrighteousness."

Every true believer wholeheartedly agrees that he is a sinner in accord with the words spoken by the apostle Paul. In so doing, He also fulfills what the Word of God is really saying in 1 John 1:9, and rejoices evermore that the blood of Jesus Christ God's Son has cleansed him from **ALL** sin. That great revelation harmonizes with every Scriptural truth found in the New Testament. Hebrews 10:14 states*: "For by one offering He has perfected forever them that are sanctified".*

The burning question raised by some believers, is this: If 1 John 1:9 simply states that we agree with God that we are sinners, what do we do when we sin if we are not to spell that sin out to God each time asking again and again for forgiveness? My dear fellow believers, in the first place there is no possible way that we can extract from that verse that common notion. In the second place the notion that we can do something to bail ourselves out, comes from the fact that we do not accept the fallen state that we are in. We refuse to agree with God, as Paul did, that we are *"carnal, sold unto sin"* (Rom. 7:14). Every one of us is in a state similar to an individual who is totally bankrupt. When we sin further, the debt ever increases and we have no resources whatsoever to pay the back debt or the ongoing debts that are on the increase every day we remain on earth.

Thank God that we have One who knew our condition before we were ever born. He knew exactly the bankrupt state which we inherited at birth. He also knew the debt that we would further incur, on a daily basis, the whole course of our lives on earth. Since all our sins were in the future when He died, our every debt was paid for to the full by His violent death on the cruel Cross. He bears the marks in His own body, to this very day, for the terrible price that He had to pay. The following quote acknowledges God's perfect justice and needs to be acknowledged and understood by every one of us, to the glory of God: *"Payment God cannot twice demand; first at my bleeding surety's hand and then again at mine."*

When we agree with God that we are in a state of total bankruptcy, incurring further debt the rest of our days on earth, our struggle in the flesh to bail ourselves out will bring us to utter despair. We will be driven to cry out, as the apostle Paul did*: "Oh, wretched man that I am! Who shall deliver me from the body of this death?"* (Rom. 7:24). When the revelation comes that we have a **Deliverer** indeed, who paid our debt to the full, all debts of the past and every debt that we may incur in the future, we can exclaim with great jubilation *"THANKS be to God through Jesus Christ our Lord ... There is therefore now no condemnation to them who are in Christ Jesus. For the law of the spirit of LIFE in Christ Jesus has made me FREE from the law of sin and death"* (Rom. 7:25 – 8:2 NASB). We should not let the chapter division interrupt the incredible truth that God reveals to us in that portion of His Holy Word. When that great revelation from God captivates our hearts, we will never again look inward to ourselves, but we will ever, from that point on, look *"unto Jesus the Author and Finisher of our faith"* (Heb. 12:2). Moreover, we will gladly accept the glorious and settled fact that *"If anyone sin we have an advocate with the Father, Jesus Christ the righteous: and He is the propitiation for our sins: and not for ours only, but also for the sins of the whole world"* (1 John 2:1,2). That grand revelation from God Himself, is directly addressed to believers. It is totally devoid of any action whatsoever on the believer's part. Our blessed Lord does it all because we are hopelessly incapable of bailing ourselves out of our bankrupt state.

The following is a quote from a Christian periodical that is widely distributed and used by a great number of believers in their daily devotions. I regret to say that what the writer states is in perfect keeping with the error I believed and taught believers for many years. He states: *"Through neglect or sin, have you **ended up by the wayside** spiritually? **Confess your sin**, repent, and **ask His forgiveness**. He is waiting to **restore you to Himself"** (underlining mine).* Amazing as it may seem, this traditional interpretation is extracted solely from 1 John 1:9. As this teaching is so widespread, it is critical that we test it with the pure Word of God that endureth forever.

Take special note of the Spirit-breathed words of the apostle Paul to the Corinthians who were sinning by joining with harlots, and note the incredible contrast. *"Now the body is not for fornication, but for the Lord; and the Lord for the body. And God hath both raised up the Lord, and will also raise up us by His own power. Know ye not that your bodies are the members of Christ? Shall I, then, take the members of Christ, and make them the members of an harlot? God forbid. What? Know you not that he that is joined to an harlot is one body? For two, sayeth He, shall be one flesh. But he that is joined unto the Lord is one spirit. Flee fornication ... what? Know ye not that your body is the temple of the Holy Spirit who is in you, whom ye have of God, and ye are not your own? For ye are bought with a price; therefore, glorify God in your body and in your spirit, which are God's"* (1 Cor. 6:13-20).

1. The sinning Corinthians were not told that they **ended up by the wayside** because of their sins. The apostle rather informed them that *"Christ died for [their] sins according to the Scriptures"* (1 Cor. 15:3). He declared that Christ would *"confirm [them] to the end that [they] may be blameless in the day of the Lord Jesus"* (1 Cor. 1:8). It could never be truthfully said that a true believer ends up by the wayside. A believer may grieve God. He may be disciplined by God, his Heavenly Father, but nowhere is it ever taught that he can end up by the wayside. The Spirit of God teaches that the

instant a believer places his trust in Christ, He has been *"delivered from the power of darkness and has [been] translated into the kingdom of His dear Son"* (Col. 1:13) From that point on his *"life is hid with Christ in God"* (Col 3:3). That is precisely why Paul was directed by the Spirit to inform the carnal Corinthians, who were going into harlots, that they would be resurrected from the dead in the same manner as their glorious Saviour (1 Cor. 6:14). These blessed truths from the Word of God, demonstrate the mighty, all inclusive work, that was forever finished for us on the cruel Cross. To Him, and to Him alone, be all the glory both now and forever.

2. As we proceed with the test, note particularly that not a word was said by the apostle of Christ to the sinning Corinthians respecting the need of **confession**, or that it was necessary for them to ask again for **forgiveness**.

3. The apostle did not tell them that **restoration** was needed. He rather revealed to them that they would be raised from the dead in the same glorious manner as their Lord (v.14). Furthermore, since they were **The temple of the Holy Spirit** (v.19), **one spirit with Him** (v.17), and **members of His body** (v.15), separation of

any kind would result in the mutilation of Christ's glorious body of which every believer is a part. The Holy Scriptures of God reveal that if we depart from His truth, and instruct sinning believers contrary to the Spirit-directed apostle, we are guilty of heresy of the worst sort.

Paul was motivated and directed by the Spirit of God, yet he never instructed sinning Corinthians or any other believers to confess their sins and ask for forgiveness. The all important question is this: why do we search in vain, yet we can never find a single instance where the Spirit-directed apostle of God ever taught believers to spell out their sins to God asking for His forgiveness? Why has the widespread teaching on confession, asking again and again for forgiveness, had such a grip on the Church for so many years? Is not the answer found in the fact that we refuse to believe that the work of our redemption was once and for all finished on the cruel Cross where *He "put away sin by the sacrifice of Himself"?* (Heb. 9:26)

I have been motivated by God to teach His Word for nearly 40 years, and I think I can safely say that most evangelical Bible teachers like to be in total agreement with their fellows. I am no exception. I feel comfortable when I research the Word and later discover that many others see the same truths that I have been shown. However, we need to remember a fact that the notable Bible scholar and teacher Campbell Morgan once stated: "Bible commentators are like sheep; they follow one another." Morgan made that statement when he was not in agreement with the commonly accepted view of Bible commentators on a certain revelation found in the Scriptures. I must say that most of us have followed one another like sheep (certainly not insincerely) in the commonly accepted interpretation of 1John 1:9, perhaps more than any other portion of the Word of God.

We should always be aware that Bible commentators have the same Bible we possess. Moreover, they have no knowledge beyond the knowledge imparted unto them by the blessed Holy Spirit. That knowledge was promised every child of God by our Saviour when He declared, *"He will guide you into all truth"* (John 16:13). Hopefully the multiplied Scriptures of truth found in this book will open our eyes to see why the commonly accepted interpretation of 1John1:9 robs the believer of the freedom into which Christ has set him free. Worse still, and far more serious, the commonly accepted interpretation tends to neutralize in our minds the finality of the work of our Saviour on the cruel Cross. It tries to rob the believer of the full, free, and final forgiveness our great God grants the instant one believes. Instead of believing and rejoicing always in God's great salvation and total forgiveness, we stop thanking Him, placing ourselves as it were, in the driver's seat, believing that **OUR** ongoing work of confession **earns** forgiveness of sins over and over again. With that forgiveness, our supposed lost fellowship with God is once again restored. Oh, how we can thank God that He has justified the UNgodly forever (Rom.4:5). He has once and for all *"called us unto the fellowship of His Son, Jesus Christ our Lord"* 1Cor.1:9, and *"God's gift and His call are irrevocable - He never withdraws them when once they are given, and He does not change His mind about those to whom He gives His grace or to whom He sends His call"* (Rom.11:29, Amp).

It is most comforting to be assured that our great God knew every move we would make and every thought that would enter our minds during our span of life on earth, even before we ourselves entered into the world. With that fact in mind we can rejoice evermore in His infallible and sure promises that everyone who receives Him as Saviour is instantly forgiven (once and for all), sealed with the Holy Spirit, and hidden with Christ in God forever. The above great truths do not call for believers to confess their sins but rather to thank God profoundly and rejoice in Him both now and forever. (1Thes.5:16).

Our Lord Jesus Himself dramatically accosted, saved, and specially chose a persecutor of the Church, Saul of Tarsus. He was singled out by God to take the rounded-out gospel to the entire Gentile world. The Word of God indicates that he was given visions and revelations even beyond what God allowed him to disclose to anyone else (2 Cor.12:4). He could say in truth, God bearing him record in the written word, *"I kept back nothing that was profitable unto you... I am pure from the blood of all men. For I have not shunned to declare unto you ALL the counsel of God"* (Acts 20:20,26,27).

When Saul of Tarsus was smitten down on the road to Damascus, our Lord gave him positive directions for the days that lay ahead: *"But rise and stand upon thy feet; for I have appeared unto thee for this purpose, to make thee a minister and a witness both of these things which thou hast seen, and of the things in which I will appear unto thee; delivering thee from the people, and from the Gentiles, unto whom I now send thee. To open their eyes, and to turn them from darkness to light, and from the power of Satan unto God, that they may receive FORGIVENESS, and inheritance among them which are sanctified by faith that is in me"* (Acts 26:16-18). That same Saul, who was later called to be an apostle, was obedient to the heavenly vision and later delivered God-breathed letters to the ones who received forgiveness of sins at the hearing of the word, *"To the Saints at Rome"*, *"To the Saints at Corinth"*, *"unto the Churches of Galatia"*, *"to the Saints who are at Ephesus"*, *"to all the Saints who are in Christ Jesus who are at Philippi"*, *"to the Saints and faithful brethren at Colosse"*, *"unto the church of the Thessalonians which is in God, the Father, and in the Lord Jesus Christ"*, but never once in all of his letters did he give the remotest inclination that they could get out of fellowship with the God whom he declared was their very life. Moreover, He gave no indication whatsoever that it was necessary for believers to confess their sins asking again and again for forgiveness. Confession with respect to sin is totally foreign to all the Spirit-directed instructions of this specially chosen apostle. We may search as we will, but we will never find a single reference to confession of sin, either in the letters to all the Churches or, for that matter, in the pastoral epistles.

In view of the above facts we have to come to the inevitable conclusion that confession of sin on the part of the believer, with its kindred teaching of supposed loss of fellowship, is not part of the counsel of God to His people. If it was indeed part of God's counsel to His people, the apostle could never have stated the recorded truth, *"I kept back nothing that was profitable unto you... I am pure from the blood of all men. For I have not shunned to declare unto you ALL the counsel of God"* (Acts 20:20,26,27). He taught truths in detail. They covered every aspect that needed to be known by the Church of God. He was led by the Spirit to sound a terrible warning to those who dared add to the rounded-out gospel he was given to preach: *"But though we, or an angel from heaven, preach any other gospel unto you than that ye have received, let him be accursed. As we said before, so say I now again, if any man preach any other gospel unto you than that ye have received, let him be accursed"* (Gal. 1:8,9).

The above Spirit-directed warning is positive proof that New Testament writers were in perfect harmony with the teaching of the apostle Paul. They neither added, nor did they subtract from the rounded-out truth that was revealed to him by the Holy Spirit. It bears repeating again that he was directed by the Spirit of God to declare in positive language: *"I kept back nothing that was profitable unto you… wherefore I take you to record this day, that I am pure from the blood of all men. For I have not shunned to declare unto you all the counsel of God"* (Acts 20:20,26,27). We should also take into account that the chosen penman (Luke) was directed by the Spirit of God to **record** Paul's words of truth in the Holy Scriptures.

Oh! that every child of God would diligently research all the truth taught by that chosen apostle. They would soon discover that confession of sin, and the possibility of forfeited fellowship on the part of the believer, is totally foreign to the proclaimed rounded-out counsel of God's truth. If there was ever the possibility of believers being severed from our great loving God, we could no more restore it than we could lift ourselves by our own bootstraps. In any case we would be too late. God's word declares that: *"When we were enemies we were reconciled to God by the death of His Son, much more, being reconciled, we shall be saved by His life"* (Rom.5:10). My dearly beloved fellow believers, we need to be reminded again and again that *"He hath saved us, and called us with a holy calling, not according to our works, but according to His own purpose and grace, which was given us in Christ Jesus before the world began"* (2Tim. 1:9).

CHAPTER 1

The Finality of God's Forgiveness at the Cross

The purpose of writing this book is to glean from the eternal revelation of God the multiple words of assurance that God's people are forgiven by Him forever the instant they receive Jesus Christ the Lord as their Saviour. Our Saviour Himself, **who is our eternal life,** enters in by His Spirit (Rev.3:20) with a positive promise that He will never leave us nor forsake us (John 14:16; Heb.13:5). When we accept **without reservation,** God's revelation that *"He hath made Him (Jesus) to be sin for us, who knew no sin: that we might be made the righteousness of God in Him"* (2Cor.5:21), it will not be difficult to understand why believers' confession is never taught anywhere in the Epistles to the Churches.

The title of this book 'Forgiven Forever' was gleaned from 1John1:9. Forgiveness in that verse is in the aorist tense in the original Greek. The aorist tense indicates a once and for all forgiveness. That truth, of course, harmonizes with every reference in the Scriptures where forgiveness is spoken of. When a sinner comes to God in confession, forgiveness is instantaneous and forever. This is also in perfect keeping with the words of our Saviour when he declared: *"He that heareth my word, and believeth in him that sent me, hath everlasting life, and shall not come into [judgment], but IS passed from death unto life"* (John 5:24). The finality of forgiveness revealed by our Saviour in that verse is irrefutable.

You will probably say, "I have been confessing my sins, asking for God's forgiveness over and over again all my Christian life." Join the crowd. So have all of us. We based our actions on that one lone verse (1John 1:9) which was primarily addressed to Gnostics of John's time. The Gnostics taught that sin affects the material body only but does not affect the spirit. Hence they would not confess (agree with God) that they were sinners and needed salvation. Instruction respecting **the believer's** need to confess his sins, asking for forgiveness, is foreign to New Testament teaching. The believer is forgiven forever the instant he receives Christ as his Saviour.

Confess your sins one to another

We should however be aware that the Word of God **does** teach that we are to *"confess [our] sins to one another, and pray for one another, so that [we] may be healed"* (James 5:16,NAS). The word translated as **confess** in the above passage is different, in the original, from the word translated as

confess as found in 1John 1:9. We have already noted that the word **confess** in 1John 1:9 simply means, **to agree with God that we are indeed sinners.**

The Greek scholar, W. E. Vine, points out that the Greek word **exomologeo** translated as **confess** in James 5:16 is a stronger word than the word **homologeo** also translated **confess** in 1John 1:9. He points out that the word used in James means *"to confess forth i.e. freely openly".* 1. This is a very important observation. The Spirit of God by employing the Greek word *homologeo* in 1John 1:9 is obviously pointing out the fact that to be a true believer one has to have a settled attitude that he is a sinner with no action implied. Whereas in James 5:16, the use of the Greek word *exomologeo* expresses action. It is a command of God. As believers, we are to spell out our agreement with God that we are sinners, not to God Himself who knew every move that we would make on earth before the foundation of the world, but to our fellow believers. This does not mean to go around broadcasting to everyone all the evil deeds we may have committed in former days, but rather if one has wronged a person, he should go in a frank, humble way and confess his sin to the person who has been injured. We witness this kind of confession in times of revival when God is moving in extraordinary ways in His people. We are bathed in His presence, all sham and hypocrisy gives way to honesty and transparency, we humble ourselves like little children, confessing our sins to one another and making right our wrongs wherever possible. This has a great effect on the Church, not only on those who hear the confession, but on the confessor who humbles himself in obedience to the Scriptures. This type of confession was practised by the apostle Paul as the following Scriptures relate: Rom.7:15-25; 2Cor.12:9,10; Eph.3:8; Phil.3:12-14; 1Tim.1:15 etc. We are not to pose before our fellow believers as though we are perfect and sinless in our walk on earth, because none of us are. The same apostle revealed by the Spirit that we are nevertheless **justified by the blood of Christ in God's sight and perfected forever.** Nothing can be more obnoxious than one who thinks his performance is acceptable to God. The apostle Paul declared a truth that applies to all of us without exception. *"I am carnal, sold under sin"* (Rom.7:14). The only goodness we possess is the One who alone is good. He dwells in every believer by His Spirit. When He has absolute right-of-way in our lives a manifestation of His righteousness is inevitable.

What we noted earlier needs to be repeated as it is an amazing and remarkable fact: Confession referred to in 1John 1:9 is **not** given as a command as it definitely is in James 5:16. We have twisted it into a command. It is rather a revealed truth that contains a promise. The inspired apostle declared, *"If we confess our sins, He is faithful and just to forgive us* (aorist tense meaning once and forever) *our sins, and to cleanse us from all unrighteousness."* Anyone who knows anything about language construction knows that the apostle was not speaking a command: he was rather stating an eternal fact from God. The first chapter of 1John is not addressed to believers as we find in all the letters of Paul, Peter, Jude and 2John. 1John chapter one applies to every son of Adam outside of Christ. Confession of sin (i.e. that is agreeing with God that we are indeed sinners) is the very first step to receiving the Saviour who comes in with a promise of total forgiveness and to abide with us forever.

What is most incredible is this: in order to keep on confessing our sins, asking again and again for forgiveness, based on the one verse alone, we had to totally ignore many positive scriptures that declare unequivocally that a sinner is saved and forgiven once and forever, the instant he receives Christ as Saviour.

All of us are legalistically bent in varying degrees. We received that trait from our fallen forefather

Adam. We respond far more quickly to legalism than we do to the absolute marvelous grace of God. In Hebrews 13:9 God gave us the only perfect formula to avoid getting entangled in legalistic heresy. His word declares: *"Be not carried about with [various] and strange doctrines. For it is a good thing that the heart be established with grace." "And if by grace, then it is no more of works; otherwise grace is no more grace. But if it be of works, then it is no more grace"* (Rom.11:6). Furthermore, when our hearts are firmly established in grace there will be no more confession to God asking for forgiveness already granted to us by His marvelous Grace. God's Word to the believer regarding sin is very, very clear: *"Likewise reckon ye also yourselves to be dead indeed unto sin, but alive unto God through Jesus Christ, our Lord"* (Rom.6:11). If we obey that command, the notion of ongoing confession, asking for forgiveness, has to be removed forever from our minds. It is to be replaced with an attitude of unending thankfulness to God who put away sin by the sacrifice of Himself.

Our Lord's very first message at the outset of His public ministry declared the purpose of His marvelous condescension and once-for-all sacrifice for our sins. Hear His words: *"The Spirit of the Lord is upon Me, because He hath anointed Me to preach the gospel to the poor; He hath sent Me to heal the broken hearted, to preach deliverance to the captives, and recovering of sight to the blind, to set at liberty them that are bruised, to preach the acceptable year of the Lord"* (Luke 4:18,19). Everyone who has trusted Christ as Saviour is born into a life of absolute freedom. It is the birthright of every believer. If we are not enjoying that freedom that was purchased for us at such great and incredible cost, all the blame lies upon ourselves. His word to the Galatians who were bewitched by the legalistic Judaizers, rings out down through the centuries of time. It is just as relevant for the believer today as it was for the Galatians in their day. *"Stand fast therefore in the liberty wherewith Christ has made us free, and be not entangled again with the yoke of bondage"* (Gal.5:1). Every believer needs to be assured beyond the shadow of all doubt, that Christ has set him free for all eternity. Every shackle is removed, every fence is down, and every bar has been broken. It is the longing and desire of God that all His people enter into this great freedom and *"rejoice evermore"* according to His command in 1Thes.5:16. By accepting the Lord and entering into this glorious freedom, we not only experience a heavenly release on our part, but on God's part we glorify His great Name. *"For of Him, and through Him, and to Him, are all things: to Whom be glory for ever"* (Rom.11:36).

A widespread teaching based on a wrong interpretation of 1John 1:9 has endured for centuries. When properly analyzed it is one of the greatest kill-joys known to the believer. It attacks his freedom and his God-given peace which was forever established for us by *"the blood of His Cross"* (Col.1:20). It robs him of the joy unspeakable and full of glory that should be his on a perpetual basis, and it ignores the **finality of God's forgiveness at the Cross.** To express it in terms of our understanding, freedom, peace, and joy unspeakable and full of glory have been placed in the bank for the continual enjoyment of every believer. The supply is everlasting and inexhaustible. The eternal Son of God took upon Himself the form of man and died a violent death to put away our sins forever. He not only made us sons of God, but He gave us total access to all of heaven's resources. He made us *"heirs of God and joint heirs with Christ"* (Rom. 8:17). The answer of the apostle Paul to the carnal Corinthians with respect to their sectarian attitude was: *"Let no man boast in men. For all things belong to you, whether Paul, or Apollos, or Cephas, or the world, or life, or death, or things present, or things to come; all things belong to you, and you belong to Christ; and Christ belongs to God"* (1Cor.3:21-23, NAS). To put it in the words of another, "All of the inexhaustible resources of deity are available to all who are available to all of the inexhaustible resources of deity." We need to quit living in self-imposed poverty, accept the truth that *"now are we the sons of God"* (1John 3:2), and cash in on our heavenly inexhaustible supply. That inexhaustible supply includes freedom, peace and joy unspeakable and full of glory. The sojourners whom Peter addressed were of like passions as we are, yet they focused on their Saviour and were continually filled with the joy of the Lord. Peter, addressing them in truth, declared, *"Whom having not seen, ye love; in whom, though now ye see Him not, yet believing, ye rejoice with joy unspeakable and full of glory"* (1Peter 1:8). They were enjoying the resources of heaven to the full by simply believing in the one who provided everything for them. They had totally accepted the fact that they were made *"heirs of God and joint heirs with Christ"* as a gift from God with no strings attached. Their constant joy in the Lord proves that they were not subjected to the legalistic teaching we are fed with today. Our loving God longs for us to take full advantage of our heavenly resources here and now. By thus doing, we too will always rejoice with a joy unspeakable that glorifies God's great name.

How many times have we, as preachers and teachers, exhorted God's people to obey His commands to *"rejoice always"* (Phil.4:4) and *"Rejoice evermore"* (1Thes.5:16)? On the other hand you have continually heard us preaching and teaching you to confess your sins to God over and over again. Strange as it may seem, we had to base our teaching on confession on one lone verse in the New Testament (1John 1:9). That verse is not a command. Have you ever wondered why you have not heard messages on the verses that are indeed commands? *"Rejoice always, and again I say rejoice", "rejoice evermore",* rather than the multiplied messages from 1John 1:9 on the supposed need to confess our sins to God?

You are probably as fully aware as I am that our God, who knows the hearts of all men, could never write to Churches in our day and declare that they are rejoicing with joy unspeakable and full of glory (1Pet.1:8). Why? Does not the answer lie in the fact that we have swallowed wrong interpretations, notions and traditions of men? God's truth sets us free. Wrong interpretations and traditions of men have the opposite effect, they gender bondage and rob us of the constant joy God commands.

Any teaching that endeavors to rob the believer of the joy God has imparted to him is not in keeping with truth. Our loving Lord expressed His longing and desire that we be filled with joy at all times.

Listen intently to His words: ***"These things have I spoken unto you, that my joy might remain in you, and that your joy might be full"*** (John 15:11). Nehemiah spoke by revelation when he declared: ***"The joy of the Lord is your strength"*** (Neh.8:10). The apostle Paul revealed by the Spirit that joy is the fruit of the Spirit (Gal.5:22). The Holy Spirit is the very life of every believer (1.Cor.6:17). We should pause and give much consideration to the Scriptures just referenced. God wants you and me to be filled with the joy of the Lord at all times. His commands to rejoice are positive, plain and eternal. A joyful Christian is a great threat to Satan's kingdom. Satan, therefore, will do everything in his power to rob the child of God of that joy-gift God has imparted to him. Jesus said Satan has come ***"to steal, and to kill, and to destroy"*** (John 10:10). We should be fully aware of Satan's devices (2Cor.2:11).

This book may be a shock to you at first, because we test the traditional view held on the matter of **believers'** confession of sin, and find that it has no support in the Word of God. However, you will soon discover that this book is loaded with liberating truths of the Word of God that inevitably set the believer free. Scripture verses are carefully spelled out with their references so that the reader can readily research each one for himself. The Bereans were commended by God because they received the

Word with all readiness of mind and searched the Scriptures daily to see whether those things were so (Acts 17:11). Their teacher was none other than the God-appointed apostle Paul. Our desire is that you search the Scriptures daily to see if the things written in this book are so. We believe that the overwhelming amount of Scriptures referenced in this book, if gladly received, and afterwards researched, will send us on our way rejoicing as we may never have rejoiced before. The Spirit-breathed words found in 1Peter chapter one, with regard to rejoicing with joy unspeakable and full of glory, will then apply to us as it did to the church of old.

The correct understanding of the finality of our Saviour's work on the Cross clashes with the widespread notion that a **believer** needs to confess his sins to God perpetually in order to enjoy ongoing forgiveness as he walks the road of life. The supposed Scriptural authority for ongoing confession is taken from 1John 1:9. Because this **interpretation** contradicts the glorious harmony of all New Testament truth respecting instant once-for-all forgiveness, we decided to bring it up at one of our home Bible studies. Everyone in the study was requested to research the New Testament and come back the following week with every Scripture that teaches confession of sin to God. I must say it surprised every one of us to learn that there is only one Scripture verse in the entire New Testament that deals with confession of sin to God. One of our researchers supplied each of us with a printout from a Bible program in his computer. The printout showed every verse in the Bible where confession of sin was referenced. That conclusive evidence quickly proved that indeed only one verse in the New Testament, 1John 1:9, makes reference to confession of sin to God.

An incredible over emphasis on one verse

Take special note of the following facts:

1. Under the New Covenant the Holy Spirit chose to limit teaching on confession of sin to God, by employing one single verse in the New Testament.

2. Our dear Lord, whose teaching we profess to follow, gave no indication whatsoever that ongoing confession and asking for forgiveness was a part of the believers' responsibility in the New Covenant relationship they are to enjoy with Him. Believers are rather to *"offer the sacrifice of praise to God continually, that is, the fruit of our lips giving thanks to His name"* (Heb.13:15). It should be noted here that true thankful praise can only proceed from a heart

that is full of the joy of God's full and free salvation. It is very significant that in this same context where we are exhorted to praise God continually, we are cautioned about false doctrine: *"Be not carried about with divers and strange doctrines. For it is a good thing that the heart BE ESTABLISHED WITH GRACE"* (Heb.13:9). Believers should ever rejoice that they *"have received abundance of GRACE* (or grace overflowing) *and the gift of righteousness"* (Rom.5:17). Abundance of grace!! Could it be any better than that? When that great eternal truth is wholeheartedly received, wrong interpretations, traditions and notions of men will be quickly rejected.

3. Paul, the chosen teacher and apostle to the Gentiles, never mentions confession of sin in all of his Spirit-breathed writing.

4. With the exception of the lone verse in 1John, the remaining Spirit-inspired writers of the New Testament are totally silent on the subject. In view of the above facts we can only come to the inevitable conclusion that confession of sin to God, asking for forgiveness, has been subtly shifted from the sinner **who has not yet accepted the Saviour,** to whom it is strictly applied, blown out of all proportion, and falsely

applied to born-again believers who are already saved to the uttermost and totally forgiven of God forever and ever. We had to conclude that that one lone verse (1John 1:9) has been misinterpreted and therefore misapplied, resulting in dreadful bondage, and robbing God's dear people of the constant joy He commands and longs for them to have at all times. How can we sidestep the incredible command: *"Rejoice in the Lord always and again I say rejoice"* (Phil.4:4)? Think of the troubled believers who honestly wonder if they have really confessed **all** to God. Their cry rings out incessantly. "How will I fare if I fail to confess my sins to God as a result of ignorance, sickness or neglect"? The sad part of it is, they can find no answer to release them from their bondage anywhere in the entire New Testament. If they, for instance, research all the inspired Scriptures written by the especially-chosen apostle Paul, the questions will remain to haunt them, as confession of sin is nowhere to be found in the extensive teaching of the apostle.

The following comments from the notable Bible teacher Dr. J. Sidlow Baxter are in perfect accord with scripture revelation: *"The Christian life was never meant to be an everlasting 'penitent form'; a continual returning of the prodigal from the far country; an incessant repetition of the publican's groan, 'God be merciful to me, a sinner.' We Christian believers, alas, are still sinners; but we are no longer merely perpetual petitioners for pardon. We have found the 'everlasting mercy' and the blood-bought 'forgiveness' which covers all our sin! Although, alas, we still grieve our Father, we are no longer prodigals; we are* **at home,** *restored to true sonship, and in filial fellowship with Him! We are no longer 'standing afar off' like the publican and distantly begging, 'God be merciful (literally, be* **propitiated***)'; for the one all-inclusive, eternally-final propitiation has now been made on our behalf, and we have entered into it!*

"All the New Testament epistles were written to Christian recipients, and they all alike assume that the new Christian standing has fundamentally changed all the relationships of those who are 'in Christ Jesus'. The standpoint is, not that we are fervently **seeking** *forgiveness but that we are* **already** *forgiven in a way which puts us on a new footing — 'even as God also in Christ* **forgave** *you' (Eph.4:32). We are not just* **seeking** *peace with God, but 'being justified by faith we* **have** *peace with God' (Rom.5:1). We are* **already** *'delivered out of the power of darkness, and translated into the kingdom of God's dear Son' (Col.1:13). We are already the restored, regenerated 'children of God' (1John 3:2).*

*We are **already** 'sealed with the Holy Spirit' as the 'earnest of our inheritance' (Eph.1:13,14)."*2

The glaring absence of confession in the New Testament

Surely it is incredibly significant that the apostle John alone (in one lone verse) was led of the Holy Spirit to speak of confession of sin to God. We may search as we will through the Spirit-breathed teaching of Paul, Peter, James, Jude, Matthew, Mark and Luke, but we will never find a word about confession to God for our sins. It should go without saying that the latter-inspired writers were also specially chosen of God to reveal His perfect will to us. They covered great and glorious truths that inevitably set men free. They sounded out profound truth respecting our relationship and responsibility toward God, but never a word about confession of sin to God, asking for forgiveness, on the part of a believer. Their silence on confession of sin to God becomes all the more glaring when we consider how frequently the Holy Spirit used the following words of truth He wanted to impress upon our minds:

'Believe' is used 115 times in the New Testament.

'Faith', 'trust', 'receive' are used 75 times.

'Salvation', 'save', 'saved' are used 106 times.

Believers are said to be **IN CHRIST** over 160 times.

The **second coming of our blessed Lord** is mentioned almost 300 times in the New Testament. There is more than one clear verse for every chapter. In fact, the second coming is mentioned eight times more often than the first coming.

An exhaustive research of every verse in the Bible that relates to confession reveals that believers under the Old Covenant (Old Testament) were commanded to confess their sins and provide a living sacrifice for the sins they confessed. Do not miss the great contrast. Under the New Covenant (New Testament) believers are told to confess Christ who has once for all and forever *"put away sin by the sacrifice of Himself"* (Heb.9:26). We will refer to this later and provide the many Scripture references that bear out this truth over and over again.

Where did believers' confession originate?

Since none of the previously referenced writers (i.e.Paul, Peter, James, Jude, Matthew, Mark, and Luke) ever mentioned believers' confession of sin to God, why is that teaching so widespread? Who would want believers to be forever occupied with themselves and their sins instead of *"looking unto*

Jesus, the Author and Finisher of [their] faith" (Heb.12:2)? Who would not want our glorious Lord to receive all the credit for His finished work on the Cross? Does not Scripture positively state that believers are *"sanctified through the offering of the body of Jesus Christ once for all"* (Heb.10:10), and *"by one offering He hath perfected forever them that are sanctified"* (Heb.10:14)? Do believers who are sanctified by the offering of the body of Jesus once for all and perfected forever by Him need to go on confessing their sins to God who has declared the believer perfect before Him in love? Do not the Scriptures plainly teach that *"He put away sin by the sacrifice of Himself"* (Heb. 9:26)? Are we to rule out literal interpretation when it comes to positive Scriptural truth? Satan, the arch enemy of God and man, would certainly try to convince us that we should. However, if God does not mean what He says, who are we to say what He does mean? His Word declares that He has hidden His truth *"from the wise and [intelligent] and revealed it unto babes"* (Matt.11:25). Babes, meaning truthful in disposition, are always open and receptive to the positive truths of Scripture. Babes take God at His word and rejoice in His promises without reservation. Babes are never guilty of applying abstract meanings to or spiritualizing the straightforward declarations of God. I would ever desire to fit into the category of a babe as described by our Lord in Matthew 11:25.

Prayerfully consider the following points with your Bible as the final authority; not some commentary of man, or even this book.

Serious points to be considered

1. Under the Old Covenant (Old Testament) believers were commanded to confess their sins to the priest and bring a live offering to be sacrificed for them (Lev.5:5,6; Lev.16). The bulls, goats, or other live creatures prescribed by God, then had to be sacrificed to **COVER** the sins just confessed by the believers. Confession of sins under the Old Covenant had to be repeated over and over again for the lifetime of the believer. They had to be followed up by never-ending **sacrifices** of innocent animals. **CONFESSION of sins committed, THEN A SACRIFICE,** was God's divine order that could never be broken under the Old Covenant, for the simple reason that the blood of bulls and goats could **NEVER** take away sins, but only cover them until sins were taken away, once and forever at the Cross. Now note the great contrast. Under the New Covenant (New Testament) believers are **never** commanded to

confess their sins, but rather they are told to confess Jesus Messiah who has **already been sacrificed once and-for-all.** With that once-and-for-all sacrifice He has not just **COVERED,** but has **TAKEN AWAY** our sins forever. Our loving God wants us to ever gaze intently upon *"the Lamb of God which [has now taken away] the sin of the world"* (John 1:29). Moreover, He wants us to accept the fact that *"we are sanctified through the offering of the body of Jesus Christ once for all"* and *"by one offering He has perfected forever them that are sanctified"* (Heb.10:10,14).

2. The most serious consideration of all is found in the fact that four gospel writers were selected by God to record the rounded-out truth taught by Jesus our Lord after His death and resurrection. There is not even a hint to be found anywhere in the gospels that our Lord taught ongoing confession of sins to obtain forgiveness after He rose from the dead and established the New Covenant relationship. His especially-chosen apostle was motivated by the Holy Spirit to proclaim that **eternal salvation** is given to the sinner the same instant he trusts the Lord Jesus as Saviour. *"Be it known unto you therefore, men and brethren, that through this man [Jesus] is preached unto you the*

FORGIVENESS OF SINS: and by Him all that BELIEVE are justified from all things, from which you could not be justified by the law of Moses" (Acts 13:38,39). Justified means that a believer is declared righteous forever by the supreme judge of the universe, God Almighty Himself. In view of the positive language in the aforementioned Scripture, who would dare deny that justification from all things is now the priceless position of all believers the instant they receive the Saviour who died for them? That marvelous pronouncement fits the believer to stand before God's Holy Throne both now and forever. That is why ongoing confession is never taught in the New Testament revelation.

3. If 1John 1:9 is indeed for the believer it is most incredible that the apostle Paul, especially and miraculously chosen to be a teacher and apostle to the Gentiles, never once instructed the sinning saints in Corinth, Galatia, or anywhere else that they must confess sins of which they were guilty. Moreover, he stated with divine authority as we have already noted, *"I am pure from the blood of all men. For I have not shunned to declare unto you all the counsel of God"* (Acts 20:26,27). When we accept the truth that Jesus our Lord *"put away sin by the sacrifice of*

Himself" (Heb.9:26), we can readily understand why the Spirit-led apostle never taught believers to confess their sins. Suffice it to say, it was not part of the counsel of God that he received. If we teach on the one hand that our Saviour put away sin forever, and on the other hand we teach that it is necessary for us to keep on confessing our sins in order to be forgiven, we are guilty of confusion of the worst sort. God's counsel is perfect. *"The Words of the Lord are pure Words: as silver tried in a furnace of earth, purified seven times. Thou shalt keep them, O Lord, thou shalt preserve them from this generation for ever"* (Psalm 12:6,7).

4. 1John 1:9 is the only verse in the New Testament that informs us that the sinner outside of Christ has to confess his sins in order to be forgiven. The use of the aorist tense in that verse proves that God's forgiveness is once and forever when initial confession is made. It is most interesting to note that warnings are sounded out frequently by scholars and teachers to never build a Bible doctrine on one verse of the Bible, and rightly so. Nevertheless, one of the most serious and critical doctrines pertaining to the believers' walk and conduct is based on this lone verse - the doctrine that believers must confess their sins on an ongoing basis. Since confession of

sins to God to obtain forgiveness is not found anywhere else in the New Testament, is it not amazing how widely spread that rule is broken today? False cults are especially infamous for building doctrine on one verse of the Bible.

5. Why is 1John 1:9 the only verse in the New Testament that indicates confession to God is necessary for forgiveness? Does not the answer lie in the fact that the apostle John does not address believers in 1John chapter one, whereas Paul and Peter, for instance, in every case start off by addressing their letters strictly to the saints of God? When we consider the dead silence on confession in all the letters of Paul, it is very evident that John's target is a company of adherents who had never been born again. In chapter five of this book we will see that John was primarily addressing a group of people (Gnostics) who were refusing to admit that they were sinners.

6. If indeed a believer has to confess his ongoing sins to be forgiven (according to the common interpretation of 1John 1:9), would not every New Testament Church be exhorted again and again to be obedient to that supposedly most important and critical command? However, there is not even a single word in regard to

confession of sins in all the letters addressed to the churches by the inspired apostle. Furthermore, the notion that ongoing confession is mandatory on the part of a believer is totally foreign to our Lord's final words to the seven churches in the book of the Revelation. Our Lord never once raised the word **confession** to His Churches. It is also commonly taught that if a believer sins, he loses fellowship with God, and that restoration can only be achieved by the believer faithfully confessing every sin. When properly analyzed, that teaching takes man's final salvation out of the hand of God and places it squarely in the hand of man. God's great **GIFT** of eternal life and His promises to keep us from falling are ignored and the great revelation in John 6:37-40,44 is also totally robbed of its marvelous meaning: *"All that the Father giveth me shall come to me; and him that cometh to me I will in no wise cast out. For I came down from heaven, not to do mine own will, but the will of him that sent me. And this is the father's will which hath sent me, that of all which he hath given me I SHOULD LOSE NOTHING, but should raise it up again at the last day. And this is the will of him that sent me, that everyone which seeth the Son, and believeth on Him, may have everlasting life: and I will raise*

him up at the last day...no man can come to me,
except the Father which hath sent me, draw
him; and I will raise him up at the last day."
Let us give God all the glory now for the finality
of His work on the cruel Cross, for it is most
certain that we will do so when we see Him face
to face, and on and on, forever, and ever.

7. As there was no direction whatsoever given by
   Paul, or any of the other chosen penmen, for
   believers to confess their sins to God, asking for
   forgiveness, the early Church must have been at
   least 60 years without that instruction, as 1John
   1:9 was not written until A.D.90-95. All the
   inspired letters, written much earlier, were
   distributed among the churches, and not a single
   word can be found in any of them respecting
   confession of sin to God on the part of born-
   again believers. Do not miss this important truth
   and fact of history. If confession of sin is
   necessary for forgiveness in order to maintain
   fellowship with God, **early church believers**
   must have been out of fellowship with God
   for the 60 years prior to John's Epistle.

8. The apostle Paul, by the Spirit, makes it crystal
   clear that he received the rounded-out gospel
   directly from God. Fourteen years later, he
   compared what he had received with Peter,

James and John (Gal 2:9). They probably spent many sessions together, and were many days comparing notes. After the sessions were over, Paul reported by the Spirit that they added nothing to what he had already received from God (Gal 2:6). Surely they must have compared notes on the supposed critical necessity of believers to confess their sins to God. How could they skip a doctrine that supposedly has such an incredible bearing on every born-again believer? We need to ask ourselves why did not Paul proclaim that supposedly critical doctrine over and over again. He was appointed by Almighty God *"a preacher, and an apostle, and a teacher of the Gentiles"* (2Tim.1:11). Paul's instructions apply to multiplied thousands of saints in the Church of God down through the centuries. He declared in positive truth, *"I am pure from the blood of all men. For I have not shunned to declare unto you ALL the counsel of God"* (Acts 20:26,27). However, confession of sins to God on the part of believers is foreign to the counsel of the chosen apostle. He rather teaches the opposite. Paul's God-given instruction to the believer is very clear: *"Reckon* (count as true) *ye also yourselves to be dead indeed unto sin, but alive unto God through Jesus Christ our Lord"* (Rom.6:11). It should be most obvious that those who are obedient to that command are never expected to confess their sins. One would be afflicted with a split personality to count on both. Surely no one could count himself dead unto sin and alive unto God while at the same time confessing his sins. *"For God is not the author of confusion, but of peace, as in all churches of the saints"* (1Cor.14:33).

9. Consider once again the instance (and there are many) where the apostle Paul had to confront carnal Corinthians regarding the heathen practice of going in to harlots (1Cor.6:15). If there was ever a time when confession of sin to God was required, here is a critical case. How does the chosen apostle handle it? Why, we may ask, does he not instruct the guilty ones to confess their sins to God immediately? Do we not teach today that this has to be the first move every born-again Christian must make in order that he be forgiven and restored to lost fellowship? Why did the chosen apostle of God, led of the Holy Spirit, rather tell them that *"he that is joined unto the Lord is ONE SPIRIT,* and *"know ye not that your body is the temple (nahos - Holy of Holies) of the Holy Spirit which is in you, which ye have of God, and ye are not your own? for ye are bought with a*

price" (1Cor.6:17,19,20). If 1John 1:9 is for the believer, surely Paul was seriously remiss. Would not **we** rather have told them that they were living with unconfessed sin in their lives and were totally out of fellowship with God?

The teaching we propagate today has a startling similarity to the teaching of the Judaizers who bewitched the Galatians in the first century. It is a glaring addition to the teaching of the apostles. We need to be reminded that our great God chose Paul to be the apostle to the Gentiles. He never told them any such thing. It can be readily observed in the recorded accounts of Holy Scripture that the Spirit of God used Paul almost exclusively to instruct born-again believers with regard to their conduct. It is most evident that He never gave the apostle Paul the modern-day doctrine of continuous confession of sin to God asking again and again for forgiveness. The teaching we propagate today respecting believers' confession is foreign to the Spirit-breathed writings of the apostle. We should also be reminded that the apostle Paul was chosen of God to reveal truth that is exclusive to the church. His inspired words will abide forever. Hear the words of Scripture on this matter: *"For this cause also thank we God without ceasing, because, when ye received the Word of God which ye heard of us, ye received it not as the word of men, but as it is in truth, the Word of God, which effectually worketh also in you that believe"* (1Thes.2:13).

10. The letter to the Romans is regarded by Bible scholars and teachers as the most complete and rounded-out revelation to the Church in the New Testament. Paul had never been to Rome, therefore his letter to that church had to include every vital truth for Christian conduct so miraculously imparted to him by Almighty God. Paul addressed his letter *"to all that be in Rome, beloved of God and called to be saints"* (Rom.1:7). Take special note that Paul never once remotely hinted that confession of sin was necessary on the part of God's saved people. Confession of sin for forgiveness on the part of believers is totally foreign to the epistle of Paul to the Romans. It is most incredible how quickly heresy is accepted when it includes a role for the flesh to play. When God made the new covenant established by the shed blood of Jesus Christ our Lord, He declared *"I will"* (Heb.8:10). This is in sharp contrast to the old Covenant in which He declared *"if ye will"* (Ex.19:5). The great liberating truth of the New Covenant is lucidly expressed in Romans 4:5: *"But to him that worketh not, but believeth on Him that*

justifieth the UNgodly, his faith is counted for righteousness." When God declared "I will" in the New Covenant, He left no room for man to perform. There is nothing left but to let Him carry out His promise, and rejoice in the great work that He is doing. *"For it is God which worketh in you both to will and to do of His good pleasure"* (Phil.2:13). Our part is to yield our members as instruments of righteousness unto God (Rom.6:13).

11. A teaching that goes hand in hand with 1John 1:9 states that a Christian loses fellowship with God the moment he sins. I would exhort those who read this book to be good Bereans and search the inspired writings of the apostle Paul to the Churches to see if this teaching can be substantiated. It can be stated most emphatically beforehand that there is not the remotest hint in the inspired writing of the apostle that a born-again believer can be out of fellowship with his God who is **one Spirit** with him. The Scripture clearly states, *"He that is joined unto the Lord is one spirit"* (1Cor.6:17). On the contrary, when the apostle confronted the Corinthians and the Galatians with the sins they were guilty of, he revealed the greatest truths that pertained to their unity with their Saviour that can be found in the New Testament. We will explore this great fact

later. If a believer is entertaining the notion that he is out of fellowship with God, he should instantly be made aware that he is a member of Christ's ***"body, of His flesh, and of His bones"*** (Eph.5:30). Satan, the devil, loves to sever that eternal relationship in our minds. For ***"when we were enemies, we were reconciled to God by the death of His Son, much more, being reconciled, we shall be saved by His life"*** (Romans 5:10). Reconciled by the death of His Son while we were still enemies. What a marvelous revelation!! When we fully accept that great truth, we can never again entertain the ridiculous notion that we can be out of fellowship with Him now, being one of His dear children. Can you think of anything more absurd? Reconciled while we were still enemies of God. Out of fellowship with Him by an act of misconduct after we become His children and are made members of His body, of His flesh and of His bones. Such an absurdity could only originate in the false notions and interpretations of men.

12. A quick check will instantly prove that the apostle Paul is directed to address all his inspired letters to the saints of God, whereas 1John chapter one is not addressed to the saints as we find is the case in all the letters of Paul to

the churches. When I go to the mail box to collect the mail, I pay particular attention to each letter I receive. Periodically my mail box contains letters that are not for myself or for my family. I immediately return such letters so that the one to whom they are addressed will receive them. In the same manner we need to be **much more alert** as to whom our Lord is particularly addressing Scriptural truth. All of God's Word is for us, but it is certainly not all specifically to us.

After careful prayer and consideration of the above 12 points, may we compare 1John 1:9 and verses in context with other Scriptures in the New Testament? A simple comparison of Scripture with Scripture will quickly determine to whom 1John chapter one applies.

"That which we have received and heard declare we unto you (the gospel of Christ which is the power of God unto salvation to everyone that believeth) *that ye* (who have not received the Saviour might do so in order that you) *also MAY have fellowship with us;* ("For what fellowship hath righteousness with unrighteousness?" 2Cor.6:14). We should be aware that righteousness is something only God can give a human being. Righteousness is not something that we do, righteousness is what we are, or are not. (See 1Cor.1:30). Every believer

under the New Covenant, ratified by our Saviour's blood, has received abundance of grace and the GIFT of righteousness (Rom. 5:17). ***and truly our fellowship is with the Father and with His Son Jesus Christ"*** (1John 1:3). (Note: to follow through 1John 1:3 read only the part in italics above).

CHAPTER 2

Fellowship with God a once-for-all call of God

May we never fail to understand that to have fellowship with God and His people we must be called by God Himself into that fellowship. The Corinthians were told in no uncertain terms that they *"were called* (by God Himself) *into the fellowship of His Son Jesus Christ our Lord"* (1Cor.1:9). It is most evident that the ones John addressed were not believers, otherwise (like the Corinthians) they too would already be called of God into the fellowship of His Son. All those who believe are Saints by God's calling and fellowshippers by God's calling. Our sainthood and our fellowship both stand on the finished work of the Cross, not on our conduct. Bad conduct, however, results in God's loving discipline of the believer who became a child of God the instant he received the Saviour. Good conduct can only be achieved by a believer yielding his members to God. For God alone is good. Our Lord Himself clearly stated an eternal truth, *"There is none good but one, that is, God"* (Matt.19:17). If indeed there is a manifestation of goodness in our lives, it has to originate from Him who alone is good. It can never be accomplished by an effort on our part. However, when we yield our members to Him, He takes over and a manifestation of righteousness is the inevitable result.

We should seriously consider what the apostle Paul declared to the Corinthians: *"And I, brethren, could not speak unto you as unto spiritual, but as unto carnal, even as unto babes in Christ...for ye are yet carnal: for whereas there is among you envying, and strife, and divisions, are ye not carnal, and walk as men?"* (1Cor.3:1,3). What more appropriate place than here could be found to teach confession for forgiveness? Did Paul miss the Spirit's leading here? Or is confession only necessary when greater sins than envying, strife, and divisions are committed? Did the Corinthians lose fellowship with God as a result of the aforementioned sins? If indeed they did, could there be a more important place to tell them so? To these very same people the apostle, by the Spirit, distinctly declared, *"God is faithful, by whom ye were called unto the fellowship of His Son Jesus Christ our Lord"* (1Cor.1:9).

God is certainly no respecter of persons (Acts 10:34). If John was addressing born-again believers in 1John 1:6,7, they too would be *"called by God unto the fellowship of His Son Jesus Christ our Lord"* (1Cor.1:9).

The Word of God the only true test

The false notion that a believer can be in and out of fellowship with God can easily be tested further by holding it up to the light of the Word of God. At the last supper our Lord announced that the cup was a symbol of His shed blood that would establish a brand New Covenant with mankind. We are plainly informed in Hebrews 10:15-18 that *"The Holy Spirit also is a witness to us: for after that He had said before, this is the covenant that I will make with them after those days, saith the Lord, I will put my laws into their hearts, and in their minds will I write them; and their sins and iniquities will I remember no more. NOW WHERE [FORGIVENESS] OF THESE IS, THERE IS NO MORE OFFERING FOR SIN."* The last sentence in that Scripture speaks volumes. The Hebrews knew only too well that under the Old Covenant, when they came to the High Priest to confess their sins, they had to have a live offering. That live offering had to pay by death for the sins they were confessing (Lev.5:5,6). When our Lord declares, *"Their sins and their iniquities* (lawless acts) *will I remember no more",* how could He now accept our confession? Since the Spirit of God witnesses to believers by the eternal word, that their sins and their lawless acts are remembered no more by God, how CAN we ignore that great truth and continue confessing our sins instead of thanking Him for that great fact?

Furthermore, since God remembers our sins no more under the New Covenant relationship, ratified by His blood alone, surely it is a great heresy to teach that a believer who sins is out of fellowship with God. We have the same blessed harmony regarding sins forgotten by God in 2Cor.5:19, NIV, where we read *"that God was in Christ reconciling the world to Himself, not counting their trespasses against them."* Since God is not counting men's sins against them, what business do we have in counting them and confessing them, asking for forgiveness? Are we not as a result of our unbelief, trying to persuade God to change His mind and restore them to His memory? Since God is not counting our sins nor retaining them in His memory, where do we get the authority to teach that His blood-purchased people are out of fellowship when they sin? Paul the apostle, led of the Spirit, commanded every saint of God at Philippi to *"Rejoice ALWAYS, and again I say rejoice"* (Phil.4:4). (He repeated the command in case they missed it the first time.) He commanded every saint in Thessalonica to *"Rejoice EVERMORE"* (1Thes.5:16). It is quite obvious that our great God, who knows the future of every saint as well as the past, never allows for a break of any kind in our fellowship with Him. If there was any possibility whatsoever in God's mind for fellowship to be broken, He would never command His saints to rejoice evermore. If there was the remotest possibility of being out of fellowship with God during our Christian walk, such a command would be a mockery. The notion that believers can be in and out of fellowship with God, depending on their conduct, is really a doctrine of works. It is nevertheless a deeply entrenched teaching of man that has the effect of nullifying the command of God to **rejoice evermore.** It also, in effect, denies that the work of our Saviour **alone** fits us to rejoice evermore in His presence. We should always understand that a believer is commanded to rejoice evermore because our Lord **finished** the work and **perfected forever** them that are sanctified by His once-for-all offering on the Cross of Calvary.

The deadly error that a child of God, cleansed and purchased by the blood of Christ, can be out of fellowship with his Lord has been broadcast and swallowed far and wide. It is yet another example of how unscriptural teaching is so readily picked up and peddled to the Christian world. There is not the remotest indication in all the letters to the Churches that fellowship with God can be lost as a result of wrong conduct on the part of a blood-bought saint.

Our God, in effect, refutes this error by choosing to reveal to the saints with the worst record of all the Churches that they were *"called unto the fellowship of His Son, Jesus Christ our Lord"* (1Cor.1:9). That call is irrevocable; *"For God's gifts and His call are irrevocable-He never withdraws them when once they are given, and He does not change His mind about those to whom He gives His grace, or to whom He sends His call"* (Rom.11:29, Amp).

God's word refutes 'in and out of fellowship'

It should be quite obvious that whoever hatched the deadly error that a saint of God can be out of fellowship with his Saviour who bought him was in effect (together with other crafty and subtle intentions) trying to refute the truth revealed in Romans 11:29. We have to go outside of the Word of God to accept the notion of 'in and out of fellowship', as it is nowhere to be found in all of the letters that are specifically addressed to the Churches of God. Our blessed Lord knew that the 'in and out of fellowship' deception would be propagated among His people. For that reason it is evident that He loaded His word with liberating truth to refute it. Hear His words of truth addressed even to the carnal Corinthians with no limitations or exceptions:

"God is faithful, by whom you were called unto the fellowship of His Son, Jesus Christ our Lord" (1Cor.1:9).

"All things are yours; and ye are Christ's, and Christ is God's" (1Cor.3:22, 23).

"Ye are washed, ye are sanctified, ye are justified" (1Cor.6:11).

"Ye are unleavened" (1Cor.5:7).

"Your bodies are members of Christ" (1Cor.6:15).

"He that is joined unto the Lord is one spirit" (1Cor.6:17).

"Your body is the temple [naos - the holy of holies] *of the Holy Spirit which is in you,...and ye are not your own, for ye are bought with a price"* (1Cor.6:19,20).

"For we being many are one bread and one body: for we are all partakers of that one bread" (1Cor.10:17).

"For by one Spirit are we all baptized into one body, whether we be Jews or Gentiles, whether we be bond or free; and have been all made to drink into one Spirit" (1Cor.12:13).

"For He hath made Him, to be sin for us, who knew no sin; that we might be made the righteousness of God IN HIM" (2Cor.5:21).

The scriptures noted above demonstrate the glorious fact that He *"put away sin by the sacrifice of Himself"* (Heb.9:26), and gave *"abundance of grace and of the GIFT of righteousness"* (Rom.5:17) to all who believe. If those positive truths to the carnal Corinthians can be twisted into the notion that they are still out of fellowship because of their carnality, Bible language has no positive meaning whatsoever. Satan would love for us to believe that lie. *"Who shall lay anything to the charge of God's elect? It is God that justifieth. Who is he that condemneth? It is Christ that died, yea rather, that is risen again, who is even at the right hand of God, who also maketh intercession for us"* (Rom.8:33,34).

If a person in the world could state truths similar to the above scriptures regarding a relationship, then turn around and with one swoop take it away by declaring that the ones to whom it applied could nevertheless be out of fellowship, people with any common sense would regard that person as a case for an insane institution. It would be double talk coming from a confused mind. Hear what the eternal Word of God has to say: *"Because we know that Christ, the Anointed One, being once raised from the dead will never die again; death no longer has power over Him. For by the death He died, He died to sin [ending His relation to it] once for all, and the life that He lives He is living to God - in unbroken fellowship with Him. Even so CONSIDER YOURSELVES ALSO DEAD TO SIN and your relation to it broken, but [that you are] alive to God - living in UNBROKEN fellowship with Him - in Christ Jesus"* (Rom.6:9-11, Amp). Every child of God who obeys the above command will be richly rewarded, for obedience to that command gives all the glory to the One who alone finished the work. On the other hand, ongoing confession of sin and asking for forgiveness can never harmonize but rather rejects the liberating truth revealed in that glorious revelation. One wonders how many of God's dear people find it impossible to obey that command because they are continually confessing their sins and begging God to forgive them. Oh, that all the people of God would accept the finality of God's Word found in 1John 2:12: *"I write unto you, little children because your sins ARE FORGIVEN YOU FOR HIS NAME'S SAKE."* That undoubtedly means sins of the past, sins of the present, and sins of the future; for all our sins were future when Christ died.

No variableness or shadow of turning with God

The all important question that every child of God

needs to know is this: DOES GOD EVER CHANGE HIS ATTITUDE WITH REGARD TO FELLOWSHIPING WITH HIS BLOOD-BOUGHT PEOPLE? Or does God's attitude change towards us every time an evil thought enters our mind, and at what point does the severance take place? We already know, only too well, that a believer's attitude CAN BE as changeable as the weather. It is only the stabilizing eternal truths of the Word of God that keep us assured of His eternal love and eternal power. False cults with their fallacious notions are ever on the job trying to cut that eternal cord that forever binds the believer with the Saviour who died for him. However, God's dear children (and especially His beloved gifted teachers) need to be assured over and over again *"That by two immutable things, in which it was impossible for God to lie, we might have a strong consolation, who have fled for refuge to lay hold upon the hope set before us: which hope we have as an anchor of the soul, both sure and steadfast, and which entereth into that within the veil; whither the forerunner is for us entered, even Jesus, made an high priest forever after the order of Melchizedec"* (Heb.6:18-20). *"Every good gift and every perfect gift is from above, and cometh down from the Father of lights with whom is NO VARIABLENESS, NEITHER SHADOW OF*

TURNING. OF HIS OWN WILL begat He us with the word of truth" (James 1:17,18). *"He hath said I WILL NEVER LEAVE THEE, NOR FORSAKE THEE"* (Heb.13:5). *"Ye are no more strangers and foreigners, BUT FELLOW CITIZENS WITH THE SAINTS, AND OF THE HOUSEHOLD OF GOD"* (Eph.2:19).

Oh, that we would stand on these great eternal words of truth; what fellowship, what joy divine, would be ours at all times, whether we performed well today or badly tomorrow. False notions of being out of fellowship because of our works would be forever banished from our minds. We need to reflect on this question: Would God restore us to fellowship at the cost of the death of His Son, then allow us to fracture it at every turn?

God's fellowship with His blood-bought children NEVER changes. That is why He informed the Church with the worst conduct of all the Churches, that Jesus Christ *"shall also confirm you unto the end, that you may be blameless in the day of our Lord Jesus Christ. GOD IS FAITHFUL,* (they were anything but) *BY WHOM YE WERE CALLED UNTO THE FELLOWSHIP OF HIS SON JESUS CHRIST, OUR LORD"* (1Cor.1:8,9).

The fallacy so widely disseminated, namely, that a believer can sever the eternal fellowship established by God on the basis of the finished work of our Saviour on the Cross, is probably the most devastating teaching that has ever entered the Church, as it affects every child of God. The great liberating truth, *"If any [one] sin, we have an advocate with the Father, Jesus Christ the righteous and HE is the propitiation for our sins"* (1John 2:1,2) which alone can set the believer free, is ignored and turned right around. It is substituted with a binding notion that the believer has to bail himself out of a sinning state by confession. The flesh loves to hang on to the act of confession. An activity, no matter how small it may be, leaves room for the flesh to perform. The flesh will never accept the finality of our Lord's work on the Cross for the simple reason that it would be signing its own death warrant. Because the flesh always wants to perform, we are more prone to look to ourselves when we fail God than we are to *"look unto Jesus the author and finisher of our faith"* (Heb.12:2). False teachers ALWAYS try to get their followers to focus on themselves rather than on the Saviour who died for them and finished the work. It started early: *"Oh foolish Galatians, who hath bewitched you, that ye should not obey the truth, before whose eyes Jesus Christ hath been evidently set forth, crucified among you?"* (Gal.3:1). The point of their departure was the forgetting of the Saviour's Cross. When the

Cross of Christ becomes dull before our eyes, room is made for false doctrine. As a matter of fact, false teaching is dead in the water until we get our eyes off the Cross. False teachers are throttled by believers who keep their eyes on the finished work of the Cross. They thrive on those who will not obey God's word to *"Reckon ye also yourselves to be dead indeed unto sin, but alive unto God through Jesus Christ our Lord"* (Rom.6:11).

Our Lord's prayer, "That they may be one, even as we are one"

The teaching that a believer whose *"life is hid with Christ in God"* (Col.3:3) can be out of fellowship with His Saviour who paid the supreme price to place him in that glorious position, is far more serious, dangerous and subtle than first meets the eye. When closely analyzed it is also a denial of answered prayer. In this particular case it, in effect, denies that our Lord's great intercessory prayer was answered by the Father. We cannot help sense the great longing and desire of our Lord for permanent never-ending fellowship with His people. He knew only too well that fallen sinful man could never bring about a reconciliation. He knew that it could only be accomplished by His own work on the cruel Cross that was now foreshadowing Him. He therefore voiced before the Father's throne a most marvelous prayer: *"That they all may be one; as Thou, Father, art in Me, and I in Thee, that they also may be one in us: that the world may believe that Thou has sent Me. And the glory which Thou gavest Me, I have given them; THAT THEY MAY BE ONE, EVEN AS WE ARE ONE: I in them, and Thou in Me, that they may be made perfect in one; and that the world may know that Thou has sent Me, and hast loved them, as Thou has loved Me"* (John 17:21-23). God the Father would have folded up the entire universe if necessary to answer that prayer.

If we teach that this marvelous divinely-arranged union that He purchased with His own blood can be gained or lost by human conduct, we are terribly deluded and need the great liberating truths of God to set us free. Once again it was to none other than the carnal Corinthians, with the worst record of all the churches, that God revealed the glorious answer to our Lord's intercessory prayer: *"FOR BY ONE SPIRIT [WERE] WE ALL BAPTIZED INTO ONE BODY, whether we be Jews or Gentiles, whether we be bond or free; and have been all made to drink into one Spirit"* (1Cor.12:13). That great revelation to the carnal Corinthians proves beyond all shadow of doubt that our Lord's intercessory prayer, *"that they may be one as we are"*, was fully and completely answered by that supernatural baptism that is inevitably shared by every believer the instant he receives Christ as Saviour. If it was not His plan to bring it to pass He would never have uttered and recorded that extraordinary prayer. Oh, what a glorious revelation! Every believer, bond or free, Jew or Gentile, regardless of denominational affiliation is one with Christ and a member of His body, of His flesh, and of His bones (Eph.5:30).

If we teach that we as believers, whom God ***"RAISED UP WITH HIM, and seated us WITH HIM in the heavenly places, IN CHRIST JESUS"*** (Eph.2:6, NAS.), who are members of Christ's body, can be out of fellowship with God, we are, in effect, teaching that Christ can get out of fellowship with the Father. The relationship of every blood-bought believer with his glorious Lord **HERE AND NOW** is **the same relationship the Father has with the Son.** The Word of God declares positively and plainly that that relationship remains unchangeable for all the ages of eternity. One has to wonder how anyone can deny that fact in the light of positive Scriptural truth. Man's notions and his attitude toward fellowship with God can be as changeable as the weather vane. Satan, the devil, loves to keep the believer focusing on himself instead of standing on the solid rock of God's great truth. However, that blessed and glorious fellowship relationship was established alone by the One who is now in heaven with the nail-pierced hands and the wounded side. *"To Him be glory both now and forever. Amen"* (2Peter 3:18). Our Lord's prayer is forever settled in heaven: *"That they may be ONE, even AS WE ARE ONE"* (John 17:22). May God have mercy on us if we try to deny that glorious eternal relationship which He purchased by His own blood. It was His obedience, and His obedience alone, that made every believer righteous and fit to stand in His presence both now and forever. *"For as by one man's disobedience* (Adam's) *many were made sinners, so by the obedience of one* (Jesus our Lord) *shall many be made righteous"* (Rom.5:19). Satan will use every imaginable trick in the book to try to put a wedge in the mind of the believer between him and His loving God. That great accuser of the brethren is relentless in his efforts to get us to focus on our flesh instead of *"looking unto Jesus the author and finisher of our faith"* (Heb.12:2). *"For the flesh lusteth against the Spirit, and the Spirit against the flesh: and these are contrary the one to the other: so that ye cannot do the things that ye would"* (Gal.5:17).

Hal Lindsey in his book *"Amazing Grace"* points out the following: *"The Greek language has many words to every one in English. It was the most explicit language ever devised in the history of the human race. I'm sure it was no mere accident that this was the language God chose for the writing of the New Testament.*

"There are three words in the Greek language expressing the idea of reconciliation, and these are translated by the one English word 'reconciliation'.

"WORD NO.1 The word **daillassomai** *means to change two people to friendship who are at odds with each other. It's used that way in Matt.5:24 '...first be reconciled to your brother, and then come and present your offering.' These two people have turned their backs on each other, both are angry and need to be reconciled. This word is never used with reference to God—we have turned our backs on God, not He on us.*

"WORD NO.2 is **apokatallasso***. It's closely aligned with the main verb we want to consider. It means to change from enmity to fellowship permanently.* (Please do not miss the Spirit's choice of words. Permanent fellowship was established by the finished work of the Cross where God crucified each child of His by placing him in Christ Jesus his Lord.) *This word also means that only one person is alienated and needs to be reconciled. The other person still loves the alienated one and needs no reconciliation. This is the word used* **with reference**

to man being reconciled to God forever. *God never needed to be reconciled.* **'For God so loved the world, that He gave His only begotten Son, that whoever believeth in Him, should not perish but have everlasting life'** *(John 3:16).*

"WORD NO.3 is **katallasso.** *This word also means* **to change from enmity to fellowship.** *It is used several places in the New Testament. It's used throughout 2 Cor.5:17-21, the key passage on reconciliation.*

*"***Katallasso*** *(reconciliation) views it this way: man is alienated from God; he turned his back on God. God never had to be reconciled, He has always sought to bring man back. Man is running from God because of guilt, and this guilt has produced a state of alienation toward God. Man believes God hates him.* **Katallasso** *focuses on God removing man's alienation* (note particularly) *and bringing him into fellowship."*[1] (Note: comments within the brackets are mine.)

When we insist on our tradition that God can be in and out of fellowship with His blood-bought people, depending on their conduct, it is another glaring instance where Scriptural truth is disregarded.

1. We have to ignore the God-breathed words so carefully chosen by the Holy Spirit as noted in the Greek text above.

2. We are in effect declaring that our loving Saviour's violent death on the Cross was not sufficient to accomplish a permanent fellowship relationship with our God who has justified us.

3. We have to ignore that the key passage on reconciliation was addressed to the carnal Corinthians who had the worst record of all the churches. Their conduct was in dire need of correction, but it did not alter or nullify in any way the fact that they were called into the fellowship of our Lord and Saviour Jesus Christ. The above points are very, very serious and critical.

CHAPTER 3

A marvelous revelation of our Lord's intercessory work

We have a most wonderful and extraordinary revelation of our Lord's intercessory work on behalf of Simon Peter, one of His chosen and called disciples. First of all, we need to be reminded that no one could be more fully informed about the mighty works of God than Simon Peter. Peter's awful sin and failure cannot be blamed on his lack of knowledge for the following reasons:

1. He walked with our Lord during the whole course of His ministry here on earth.

2. He was one of the inner circle (Peter, James and John) who saw every extraordinary miracle Jesus performed.

3. He saw the power and coming of our Lord when he was with Him on the holy mount. (cf Matt.16:28 -17:9 with 2Peter 1:16).

4. He sat under our Lord's teaching for three and one half years, yet at the end he deliberately lied, denying that he ever knew Him. In his third denial he resorted to cursing and swearing (Matt. 26:74). However, hours before he sinned so grievously, ***The Lord said, Simon, Simon, behold, Satan hath desired to have you, that he***

may sift you as wheat; but I have prayed for thee, that thy faith fail not: And when thou art converted [turned again] strengthen thy brethren" (Luke 22:31,32). Oh, what an incredible window of truth into this critical and mysterious area. This marvelous insight into **our Saviour's work of intercession** should speak volumes to every believer. While Simon was still boasting how he was sure to hang in there, our blessed Lord had already interceded for three terrible sins he was going to commit in the future. When we consider **our Lord's reaction** to the terrible sins Simon was about to commit, and compare it with the incredible emphasis today on the supposed necessity of confession and loss of fellowship, the only true conclusion possible is this: we are confronting another gospel (Gal.1:6). If there was ever a critical incident where confession and supposed loss of fellowship needed to be taught, here is the place. Our blessed Lord, however, never instructed Peter to confess his sin. Furthermore, detailed accounts in Scripture demonstrate that our Lord had totally forgiven Peter and had interceded for him long before his sinful acts were ever committed. He also sought out Peter immediately after He rose from the dead, proving that His longing and desire for Peter's fellowship never varied in spite of Peter's awful denial. We need to search the Scriptures and take special note of how the great truths of the Bible here, and in many other places, refute the terrible notion that a believer called by God into His fellowship, purchased by our Saviour's finished work on the Cross, can lose that precious fellowship by his action or conduct.

1. In reply to Peter's question, *"Lord whither goest thou?"* and to his boast that followed that question, *"I will lay down my life for thy sake",* Jesus responded directly to Peter and said, *"Wilt thou lay down thy life for my sake? Verily, verily, I say unto thee the cock shall not crow, till thou hast denied me thrice"* (John 13:36-38). After revealing that shocking truth to Peter, blessed be His name, He went on to say to Peter, *"Let not your heart be troubled: ye believe in God, believe also in me. In my Father's house are many mansions: if it were not so, I would have told you"* (John 14:1,2). Getting back to Peter's question of John 13:36 *"Where goest thou?"* He continues by saying to Peter, *"I go to prepare a place for you, and if I go to prepare a place for you, I will come again and receive you unto myself, that where I am, there ye may be also."* We must not let the chapter division (13&14) rob us of the fact that our Lord's reply

to Peter continues without a break into the 14th. chapter. Chapter divisions were inserted centuries after Jesus, our Lord, spoke these words to Peter. History records that chapter divisions were inserted in the 13th century, 1248 A.D. to be exact. Peter's questions and our Lord's direct response to them begin at John 13:36 and end at John 14:4. Our Lord no doubt gave the great revelation of His going away and glorious return directly to Peter to reinforce and comfort him, knowing that he would desperately need assurance and comfort after his terrible denial that was soon to follow. We need to be assured, however, that that marvelous revelation of our Lord's glorious return, though directed to Peter in answer to his question, nevertheless applies to all believers. It is blessed and also wonderful to take special note that our Lord said to Peter, *"Let not your heart be troubled"* immediately after informing him of his terrible denial that was soon to follow. Amazing Grace!

2. After revealing to Peter the shocking truth that he would deny him three times, the Scriptures relate that they departed to the Garden of Gethsemane where Jesus would soon be arrested. Who would we choose to be nearest to us if we faced impalement on a cross as a result of wicked men who falsely accused us? Would

we choose one whom we knew for certain would shortly deny that he ever knew us? Oh, my dear reader, when we say or even think that our Lord severs fellowship with His believers because of bad conduct on their part, we do not know what we are talking about. The Scriptures state: *"Then cometh Jesus with them unto a place called Gethsemane, and saith unto the disciples, sit ye here, while I go and pray yonder. And He took with Him PETER and the two sons of Zebedee, and began to be sorrowful and very heavy. Then saith He unto them, My soul is exceeding sorrowful, even unto death: tarry here, and watch ye with Me"* (Matt.26:36-38).The very one whom Jesus knew would deny Him three times with cursing a short time later is Jesus' top choice to be with Him in the hour of His greatest trial and agony. This God-breathed revelation strikes a death blow to the notion of loss of fellowship and need of confession to have it restored. Surely this infallible record points out that our Lord's attitude to Peter never changed one iota. His love and desire for Peter's fellowship was as keen and as constant as if Peter had remained true and faultless to the very end of his days on earth.

3. With reference to the record of Peter's actual denial, four gospels record the details. When

Peter denied for the third time, with cursing and swearing (Mark 14:71), *"The Lord turned, and looked upon Peter. And Peter remembered the word of the Lord, how He had said unto Him, Before the cock crows, thou shalt deny me thrice. And Peter went out and wept bitterly"* (Luke 22:61,62).

Perhaps it is too sacred to even guess what was involved in that look. However, God's Word informs us *"that the goodness of God leadeth thee to repentance"* (Rom.2:4). Therefore, we can rest assured that our Lord communicated love, compassion, mercy and total forgiveness by that look. It so overwhelmed Peter that he went out and wept bitterly. When anyone gets a real glimpse of our Lord's great love and exceeding grace, it has the same effect as it had on Peter. We are prone to bring God Almighty down to our level of thinking. However, our loving God has declared: *"For My thoughts are not your thoughts, neither are your ways My ways, saith the Lord. For as the heavens are higher than the earth, so are My ways higher than your ways, and My thoughts than your thoughts"* (Isaiah 55:8,9). Even a loving human mother would never sever fellowship with a disobedient child. Such a notion would never enter her mind. Keeping that in mind, we can see how our Lord, whose ways are higher than our ways as the heavens are above the earth, demonstrated so clearly in His attitude toward Peter that a severance of fellowship with Peter never entered His mind in spite of Peter's sin and awful denial. When we consider it from a human perspective we wonder how our Lord could even tolerate Peter when He knew he would sin and fail Him so terribly. The answer is found at the Cross, where His great love was demonstrated, when He *"bare our sins* (and Peter's) *in His own body on the tree, that we, being DEAD TO SINS,* (note how God views the believer) *should live unto righteousness: BY WHOSE STRIPES YE WERE HEALED"* (1Peter 2:24).

4. We have a further revelation of our Lord's immutable attitude toward Peter, in spite of his denial, in the inspired gospel accounts. We note with awe that Peter was the only one our risen Lord singled out and named after He rose from the dead: *"Tell His disciples and Peter"* (Mark 16:7). Furthermore, our Lord had a special visit with Peter **first, before He appeared to any of His other apostles.** Peter had the priceless privilege of being the **first of the apostles** to enjoy a special visitation from our Lord after His resurrection (Luke 24:34). The divinely inspired

record of our Lord's consistent attitude toward Peter repudiates the common notion that a believer is severed from fellowship because of sin and failure in his life. May we repeat again that fellowship is a calling of God (1Cor.1:9) according to His sovereign will. God can righteously call into fellowship whosoever He will, on the basis of the finished work on the Cross where Jesus our Lord tasted death for every man (Heb. 2:9). It would appear that the notion of broken fellowship is designed by the enemy to put a wedge between the blood-purchased believer and his loving Lord.

We would have to be very blind indeed, to miss the divine consistency of our Lord's desire for fellowship with Peter both before and after our Lord's cruel death on the Cross. I am sure that the inspired record was designed to demonstrate to every believer that God longs to fellowship with His purchased people regardless of their sins and their failures, because all their sins and their failures were taken care of on the cruel Cross. The Spirit-inspired account of Peter's sin and failure, coupled with the details of our Lord's immutable attitude toward Peter, should speak volumes to every believer. The revelation of our Lord's obvious consistent desire to have fellowship with Peter, both before and after his sinful failure, strikes a death blow at the deadly notion that severance of fellowship occurs when a believer sins. Did our Lord deviate from His righteous standards and make an exception of Peter? (see James1:17). Is God a respecter of persons? (see Acts 10:34).The truths of scripture demand a categorical no! to both questions. What a marvelous and wonderful comfort, therefore, to know that our loving Lord moves into action, as he did for Peter, long before we ever commit an act of sin. What glorious harmony, also, with His word to us in 1John 2:1 *"My little children...if any [one] sin, we have an advocate with the Father, Jesus Christ the righteous"*. We are not told to make the move. He Himself intercedes on our behalf, as He did with Peter, long before the act occurs. My dear reader, all that we can do is continually thank Him both now and forevermore, for it is *"the goodness of God that leadeth [us] to repentance"* (Romans 2:4).

CHAPTER 4

The believer is born into God's fellowship estate

Fellowship is a calling of God alone. It was righteously established by our Saviour's finished work on the Cross. It is the birthright of every believer. To be called into the fellowship of God is similar to being born into a world full of oxygen for us to breathe. It is God's provision alone. If we are smothering for want of oxygen, all we need to do is breathe it in. If we want fellowship with God as born-again redeemed believers, all we need to do is start enjoying it. It is as free and as available as the oxygen all around us. This is an area where we need to be transformed by the renewing of our minds. The truth received by us and implanted by God effects the great transformation. We were dead in trespasses and sins when our loving God called us into His glorious fellowship estate. We had no lot or part in it, other than to receive it. When we did receive the Saviour, a marvelous translation took place. The mighty power of God went into action. We were instantly translated out of the kingdom of darkness and placed into the kingdom of God's dear Son (Col.1:13). That is why the apostle was directed by the Spirit to command the Galatians, who had been bewitched into not obeying the truth, to *"stand fast therefore in the liberty wherewith Christ [had] made [them] free"* (Gal. 5:1). There was nothing they had to do to get back into fellowship. **They were already in fellowship** as born members of the family and household of God. Self-appointed teachers (Acts 15:24), ignorant of God's all inclusive provision for every believer, succeeded in twisting their minds into thinking that there was an activity on their part to maintain God's eternal relationship with them. When they fell for that deadly error, they shifted their focus from their glorious Deliverer to themselves. They needed a fresh infusion of truth to flush out that deadly error in order that they begin to breathe in the fellowship, the freedom and the all-encompassing love that was already theirs in the kingdom wherein they were dwelling. Sad to say they were unaware that they were already seated together in heavenly places in Christ Jesus their Lord (Eph. 2:6). Oh, how they needed to be made aware that they were delivered from the power of darkness, and translated into the kingdom of God's dear Son (Col.1:13). That glorious translation was effected the instant they placed their trust in the Saviour. The apostle's instruction to them was clear and precise: **There was nothing whatsoever on their part that had to be done, except to stand fast in what was already once and for all and forever given to them by their loving God.**

In view of the extraordinary emphasis that is placed on Christian confession today, we marvel that the word 'confess', or for that matter, 'confession' is never mentioned once in Paul's Spirit-breathed directions to the 'foolish' Galatians or to the 'carnal' Corinthians. It is all the more amazing when we take into consideration that Paul was brought up under the **Old** Covenant that demanded perpetual confession of sin. Paul must have confessed his sins hundreds of times before he was converted to Christ and entered into the New Covenant. Along with his confession under the Old Covenant, he had to provide a live offering to be slain for the sins he committed (Lev.5:5-6). Paul, like all faithful Jews, was also accustomed to confessing his sins and fasting on the regular Day of Atonement. Nevertheless, he is totally silent on the matter of confession to sinning believers who are under the **New** Covenant.

Had I been present when Paul wrote his letter to the Galatians, I would have told them in no uncertain terms that they **must** search their hearts. They were out of fellowship, and could never be restored until they confessed every sin they had committed and asked God to forgive them. If the notion I once held prevailed in Paul's day, he no doubt would have been led to rebuke it with greater intensity than the first heresy of the Galatians.

The unity of God and the believer is eternal

With the same positive language the Corinthians were informed that they were called (by God) into the fellowship of His Son. These same carnal Christians (1Cor.3:1-3) were also informed that *"He that is joined to the Lord is one spirit"* (1Cor.6:17). The letter to the Hebrews reveals a similar marvelous truth: *"He that sanctifieth and they who are sanctified are ALL OF ONE"* (Heb.2:11). In the letter to the Colossians, all believers are told: *"Ye are dead, and your life is hid with Christ in God"* (Col.3:3). The Word of God further declares that believers are *"members of His body, of His flesh, and of His bones"* (Eph.5:30). Even a casual reading of the above eternal truths shows up the subtleness of the 'in and out of fellowship' teaching. It endeavors to make a mockery of the positive truths of God. Where does anyone find authority to teach that it is possible to be out of fellowship with our great and wonderful God who Himself called us into that fellowship? (1Cor.1:9). Where, pray tell me, is there a Scripture that declares we can be in and out of fellowship with God depending on our faulty walk? Could one be out of fellowship with God who is one spirit with Him? (1Cor.6:17). Could one be out of fellowship with one's own life? The

Word of God positively declares that Christ is our life (Col.3:4). Could we say on the one hand, I was crucified with Christ and it is no longer I who live, and at the same time accept the notion that I am out of fellowship with God? (Gal.2:20). If indeed we can be out of fellowship with God and need by confession to be forgiven and restored, why didn't Paul, the chosen apostle of God, teach the carnal Corinthians that supposed truth? Why didn't Paul teach the Galatians the same?

If the commonly taught notion that ongoing confession is necessary for cleansing and forgiveness on the part of believers, the Corinthians and the Galatians must have remained in their sins, as the apostle gave them no instructions to do so. Could the Corinthians undo the fact that they were saints by God's calling? (1Cor.1:2). Could the Corinthians undo the fact that they were called by God into fellowship with His Son, Jesus Christ our Lord? (1Cor.1:9). If indeed they could undo the one, surely they could also undo the other. The same word in the Greek original is used for 'calling' in both instances.

Confession of sin for the restoration of supposed loss of fellowship very subtly places man as the initiator of the work. Man is determined that he is going to have some part in his own salvation one way or another. Ongoing confession of sin gives the flesh just what it thrives on, a continuous work to perform. There is a fleshly satisfaction in confession that man does not want to give up. That is why confession boxes are crowded with adherents. It has been going on down through the centuries, since the outset of the dark ages. It makes us feel good because we have completed a performance. We have added another fig leaf to our own covering. Our blessed Lord, however, has declared most plainly the only work He ever wants us to perform: *"This is the work of God that you believe on (rely on, trust in) Him whom He hath sent"* (John 6:29). Rom.4:5 reveals the same truth: *"But to him that worketh not, but believeth on him that justifieth the ungodly, his faith is counted for righteousness"*. Oh, if we could only grasp the necessity of just simply trusting God alone for everything.

When we sin, the Creator and upholder of the universe, our Advocate (lawyer), goes to bat for us according to His estimate of our sin (1John 2:1). That glorious revelation is beyond our human comprehension. He knows when we will sin before the thought ever enters our minds. He demonstrated that fact in the record of Peter's sin. Thank God that He ever liveth to make intercession for us according to God's estimation of the magnitude of our sins. He bears the wounds and the scars of the very sins for which He intercedes. They are an eternal manifestation of the truth that *"He was wounded for our transgressions, He was bruised for our iniquities: the chastisement of our peace was upon Him; and with His stripes we are healed"* (Isa.53:5). May we never be guilty of entertaining the notion that God demands payment twice.

The believer delivered from the power of Satan, forgiven and sanctified

Furthermore, even before the foundation of the world (from an eternal perspective), and after His glorious resurrection (from a temporal perspective), our Lord miraculously chose, saved, energized and sent forth a special apostle to the Gentile world. He filled him with His Spirit, and flooded him with the rounded-out truth to be taught to the entire Jewish and Gentile community. His message to that chosen apostle was again clear and precise: *"I have appeared unto thee for this purpose, to make thee a minister and a witness...delivering thee from the people, and from the Gentiles, unto whom now I send thee, to open their eyes, and to turn them from darkness to light, and from the power of Satan unto God, that they may receive FORGIVENESS OF SINS, and inheritance among them who are sanctified by faith that is in*

Me" (Acts 26:16-18). The same apostle was obedient to the Lord's command and declared, *"Be it known unto you, therefore, men and brethren, that through this man is preached unto you THE FORGIVENESS OF SINS; and by Him ALL THAT BELIEVE are justified from ALL THINGS, from which ye could not be justified by the law of Moses"* (Acts 13:38,39). Our dear Lord could not have made His word any plainer. Forgiveness is granted once and for all and forever in an instant of time. *"This cup is the New [Covenant] in my blood which is shed for you"* (Luke 22:20). Teaching that promotes confession of sins, asking for forgiveness, for the believer now justified is a subtle addition to the eternal Word of God. It is only too evident that it is an attempt to deny the great fact that God justifies the UNgodly (Romans 4:5).

The apostle Paul was also selected to record the rounded-out truth that was destined to reach the four corners of the globe. He was not permitted to write **even a single word** respecting the so-called necessity of saints to confess their sins. If we teach otherwise, surely we are guilty of a binding fallacy of the worst sort. That fallacy has an incredible binding effect on every child of God that receives Him as Saviour. If we insist on an interpretation of 1John 1:9 that is totally out of harmony, and even adds to the teaching of our dear Lord and His chosen apostle and gospel writer, we need to get on our knees before God and ask Him to open our eyes to the great liberating truths that inevitably set His people free.

There is no liberty, but rather bondage, in the notion that we need to continually analyze ourselves and confess our sins. That is why the sinning Galatians were never instructed to confess their sins. They were told rather to stand fast in the liberty wherewith Christ **had already set them free.** Thank God that they were not subjected to our modern notion of ongoing confession and asking for forgiveness. Forgiveness is a once-for-all pardon from God that endures forever. It is not based on our conduct, good or bad, but on the finished work of our Lord on the Cross. *"Not by works of righteousness which we have done, but according to His mercy He saved us, by the washing of regeneration, and renewing of the Holy Ghost; which He shed on us abundantly through Jesus Christ our Saviour"* (Titus 3:5,6), *"who hath saved us, and called us with an holy calling, not according to our works, but according to His own purpose and grace, which was given us in Christ Jesus before the world began"* (2 Tim.1:9).

Following on in 1John 1:6, *"If we* (human creatures) *say that we have fellowship with Him, and walk in darkness, we lie,* (as a child of God is delivered from the power of darkness and is translated into the Kingdom of God's dear Son (Col.1:13). Note - only those born from above have been translated into that kingdom of light. Those who were still walking in darkness, declaring that they were in fellowship with God, were liars because they had not received the Saviour who alone can effect that translation. Believers are clearly told that they 'were once darkness, but now you are light in the Lord' (Eph.5:8). 'Ye are all the children of light, and the children of the day; we are not of the night nor of darkness' (1Thes.5:5). The apostle John could not use that positive language in 1John Chapter1 because he was not addressing believers exclusively as Paul was) *and do not the truth* (for true believers cannot have Christian fellowship with liars). *"But if we* (human creatures) *walk in the light as He is in the light* (it proves we are not liars but born again believers) *we have fellowship one with the other, and the blood of Jesus Christ cleanseth us (KEEPS ON CLEANSING US - Greek) from ALL SIN."* (Note: To read 1John 1:6 in continuity, read words in italics only.)

It should be noted here that the original Greek in 1John 1:6 indicates that the cleansing of the blood is an ongoing activity. However, note the contrast. In

1John 1:9: *"He is faithful and just to forgive us our sins"*. The Greek sentence structure in that verse indicates God's forgiveness is once and for all. The grammatical tense in the original Greek was carefully selected by the Holy Spirit in order that it harmonize with the once-and-for-all forgiveness received by the sinner the instant he believes.

The apostle was addressing all those who had received the Saviour according to 1John 1:9 when he declared, *"I write unto you, little children because your sins are forgiven you for His name's sake"* (1John 2:12). The verb in the original Greek is in the perfect tense in this verse which speaks of a past completed action. May His name ever be praised by every reader of this book.

CHAPTER 5

Enter the Gnostics

History records that Gnostics, a cult group in the early church, were the major philosophical movement of the Roman Empire. Gnosticism was a blending of all the religious thought that existed at that time, a blending of Greek, Roman, Eastern and Indian religions.

The Encyclopedia Britannica states that Gnosticism was *"a movement of religious synchronism (or fusion of different and previously independent beliefs), which maintained itself side by side with genuine Christianity as the latter was gradually crystallizing into the ancient Catholic Church."1.* The author of the (Gnostic) **Gospel of Mary** interprets the resurrection appearances of Christ as visions received in dreams or in **ecstatic trance.** 1. The (Gnostic) **Gospel of Philip** ridicules ignorant Christians who take the resurrection literally. 2. Some Gnostics called the literal view of the resurrection "the faith of fools". The Encyclopedia Britannica states *"The conception of a resurrection of the* body, *of a further existence* of the body *after death, was unattainable by almost all Gnostics".* 3.

We should not miss the God-breathed writing in

1John 1 verses 1&2 where John, by the Spirit, very obviously and emphatically refutes the above Gnostic heresy by elaborating on the fact that they were able to touch and handle our Lord's body after His resurrection. He writes: ***"That which was from the beginning, which we have heard, which we have seen with our eyes,*** (not in ecstatic trance as stated by the Gnostics) ***which we have looked upon, AND OUR HANDS HAVE HANDLED, OF THE WORD OF LIFE** for the life was manifested, and **WE HAVE SEEN IT,** and bear witness, and show unto you that eternal life, which was with the Father, and was manifested unto us"*.* The apostle is referring to that glorious moment when our Saviour appeared to His disciples after His resurrection. Luke chapter 24:38-43 records that He insisted that they gaze intently upon Him, and touch Him, in order that all doubts, concerning the reality of His resurrection, would be removed from their minds forever.

Basically, the Gnostics believed in the separation of matter and spirit; matter was evil whereas spirit was both divine and good. One of the consequences of this belief was that it was impossible for God to become flesh and walk among us in the person of Jesus Christ. J.Vernon McGee writes: *"One of their heretical teachings was that Jesus was merely a man when He was born. He was just like any other human being at His birth, but at His baptism, the Christ came upon Him, and when He was hanging on the cross, the Christ left Him. John refutes this teaching in no uncertain terms when* (addressing the unsaved Gnostics) *he declared in his gospel record, 'The Word was* **born** *flesh'. And here in his first epistle, he emphatically declares that after Jesus came back from the dead, he was still a human being (being the God man). John says 'we handled Him' (1John 1:1) - He was still flesh and bones."4.* (Comments in brackets are mine.)

The Gnostics were concerned with the intellectual question of the origin of evil instead of the practical question of "What must I do to be saved?" Furthermore, their knowledge was based on mystic revelation, not on the Word of God. Their beliefs had practical consequences as well because they believed both that **the spirit was good and that there was no capacity for sin in it, they had no need for faith and deeds.**

Understanding the Gnostic heresy makes us realize why the apostle John had to say, *"If we say that we have no sin, we deceive ourselves, and the truth is not in us...If we say that we have not sinned, we make him a liar, and his Word is not in us"* (1John 1:8,10). Therefore, we see that the apostle John was addressing the Gnostic heresy within Chapter one. 1John chapter one could never apply to a believer. The blessed Holy Spirit, who comes to dwell within, shows up our sinful desires that will remain in us until we leave our bodies and are joined with Christ in heaven. Every believer is painfully aware that he has sin, and also that he has sinned. He can join wholeheartedly with the apostle Paul who declared, *"For I know that in me (that is, in my flesh), dwelleth no good thing: for to will is present with me, but how to perform that which is good I find not"* (Romans 7:18). *"This is a faithful saying, and worthy of all acceptation, that Christ Jesus came into the world to save sinners; of whom I am chief"* (1Tim.1:15).

The International Standard Bible Encyclopedia states: *"It may be asserted as beyond question* (take special note) *that the peril against which The Epistle* (of 1John) *was intended to arm the Church was the spreading influence of some form of Gnosticism. The pretensions of Gnosticism to a higher esoteric knowledge of divine things seems to be clearly referred to in several passages. In 2:4,6,9, e.g. one might suppose that they are almost verbally quoted ('He that saith'; 'I know Him'; 'I abide in Him,' 'I am in the light'). When we observe, moreover, the prominence given throughout to the idea of knowledge and the special significance of some of these passages, the conviction grows that the writer's purpose is not only to refute the false,* (Gnostic teaching) *but to exhibit apostolic Christianity, believed and lived, as the true Gnosis - the Divine reality of which Gnosticism was but a fantastic caricature."*5. (Comments in brackets are mine.)

A new believer is soon aware of his evil desires

1John 1:8, states ***"If we say we have no sin we deceive ourselves."*** Such a statement to believers would be superfluous. A believer could never entertain that deadly error of Gnosticism. The Gnostics taught that "we do not have any principle of sin within us, since matter is evil and the soul is not contaminated by sinful flesh". If one has indeed received Jesus as Lord and Saviour, the Holy Spirit has come to take up residence within. His Holy presence within alerts the believer, as never before, to the sinful desires within him. Some time after his so-great salvation, the new believer, who now has God's law written in his heart and on his mind, becomes painfully aware that: ***"The flesh lusteth against the Spirit, and the Spirit against the flesh"*** (Gal.5:17). Before the Holy Spirit of God entered his life, he was not sensitive to the sins he now sees in his members. As a result of the awful sins he now sees in himself, he begins to question if he was indeed saved in the first place. That is why our loving God hammers away with relentless consistency, declaring multiplied truths as to the finality of our Saviour's work on the Cross. That is also why the apostle John was led of God in 1John 2:1 to single out the children of God and inform them *"If any [one] sin, we* (John includes himself) *have an advocate with the Father, Jesus Christ the Righteous."*

The importance of rightly dividing the Word of truth cannot be over-stressed. The first chapter of 1John is NOT addressed specifically to the born-again child of God, but was designed to correct the terrible errors of the Gnostics who were bold to declare that they had no sin. The second chapter most definitely is addressed to the believer, as the writer states in the very first verse: *"My little children".* The Holy Spirit of God, now resident within the believer, not only makes him sensitive to the sin in his members, but abundantly assures him in the Word of God of the finality of the work of his Saviour on the Cross. False cults are relentless in their efforts to minimize the glorious finished work of our Saviour who suffered and died for every sin we have ever committed, sins of the past, sins of the present and sins of the future. False cults will never admit that a sinner is given ***"abundance of grace and of the GIFT of righteousness"*** (Rom.5:17) the instant he places his trust in Christ as Saviour. They never cease to try to find a part for the flesh to play. True believers should avoid, at any cost, every vestige of their heresy.

My dear reader, we will be greatly rewarded if we meditate long on Romans 5:17. ***"Abundance of grace and of the GIFT of righteousness"*** could only be given to a people who are totally forgiven for all eternity. All that we can do is thank Him forever. Think of it!! A priceless gift apart from our works, apart from the law, apart from ordinances, and apart from our worthiness. An out and out gift given directly from almighty God Himself who loves us with a love that can never be measured. The apostle Paul was given that extraordinary revelation to pass on to all those who have received Jesus Christ as their Saviour. To ignore that great revelation and go on confessing our sins, asking for forgiveness, is really a terrible insult to God. That is why we **NEVER** find teaching on confession in any of the Spirit inspired revelations given to the apostle Paul. The truth of God's glorious grace is always consistent. It will flow forth forever in wonderful harmony.

Consider the following quote from W. R. Newell:

*"Because the once for all putting away of sin forever from God's sight (Heb.9:26) is so seldom and so feebly grasped by Christian believers, these Levitical oft-repeated sacrifices are taken as setting forth Christian experience. Thus, even our Lord's priesthood, in the heart of hearts of most believers, is somehow connected with atonement. If it were told to the average real Christian, 'Jesus in heaven will never put away another sin for you,' it would strike him with real terror: for he has not rested in that once for all putting away sin at the Cross concerning which Christ said "IT IS FINISHED."*4.

The first chapter of 1John in its entirety evidently addresses those who needed salvation and deliverance from the cult known as Gnosticism. ***"...to open their eyes, and to turn them from darkness to light,*** (the inevitable result of receiving the Gospel cp. 1John1:6) ***and from the power of Satan unto God, that they may receive forgiveness of sins, and an inheritance among them who are sanctified by faith that is in [Christ]"*** (Acts 26:18). Note that release from Satan's grip, turning from darkness to light, forgiveness of sins, and sanctification are received in one package and is a work of God in its entirety. The Gnostics were in desperate need of that work to take place in their hearts. They needed to be turned from darkness to light by the power of Christ who alone can effect

that supernatural translation the moment we receive
Him as Saviour.

Believers singularly addressed

**May it be repeated over and over again that
John immediately singles out believers as we
move into the second chapter of his letter.** Note
the great contrast - to the unsaved Gnostics and to
unbelievers who had been misled by their heresy, he
does not give a command but states two facts: *"If
we confess our sins, He is faithful and just to
forgive us our sins, and to cleanse us from all
unrighteousness. If we say that we have not
sinned, we make Him a liar, and His word is not in
us"* (1John 1:9,10). May we also repeat again that
the Greek original in 1John 1:9 uses the aorist tense
indicating a once-and-for-all act of forgiveness by
God?

To the born again believer (1John 2:1,2) He
declares, *"My little children,...if any [one] sin, we
have an Advocate (a Lawyer) with the Father,
Jesus Christ the Righteous"* to handle it for us.
There is not a word about confession and certainly
not a word about asking for forgiveness. Further on
in the chapter he singles out newborn babes in
Christ and declares: *"your sins ARE FORGIVEN
YOU for His name's sake"* (1John 2:12).

The harmony of the word of God is most amazing.The present day teaching that a believer has to confess and ask forgiveness every time he sins, is really a doctrine of works that nullifies the truth that **God forgives, once and for all and forever,** the individual who confesses, or agrees with God, that he is a sinner. Oh, that we could fully grasp the marvelous truth that Jesus, the Lord of Glory, is our lawyer, our attorney, the one who laid down His very life for us. He is all-powerful, all-wise, all-knowing and everywhere present. He is at this very moment upholding all things by the word of His power and He loves us with a love that is beyond human comprehension. An old adage ought to be considered here: "The one who insists on being his own lawyer, has a fool for a client." Since the world considers a man a fool who does not take advantage of a mere man trained in law to defend him, how much greater a fool who will not leave his case entirely to the all wise Lord of Glory who died for him.

Rightly dividing the Word of Truth

Before we go further in this book would you please pause and reflect while we do another test of the inspired Holy Scripture in order that we *"rightly divide the Word of Truth"* (2Tim.2:15)? Consider

1John chapter one. Once again, take special note that it is not addressed to believers as we find in all the letters of Paul, the letters of Peter, the letter of Jude and the letter of 2John. Since 1John chapter one is not addressed to a particular church or to a particular believer, it should be a foregone conclusion that it applies to the Gnostics of that day, and to all unbelievers outside of Christ who refuse to confess that they are indeed sinners.

Turn now to the second epistle of John where we find in verse one that his second letter, (like the letters of Paul, Peter and Jude) is specifically addressed to believers. He writes:*"The elder unto the elect lady and her children, whom I love in the truth; and not I only, but all they that have known the truth; for the truth's sake, WHICH DWELLETH IN US, AND SHALL BE WITH US FOREVER"* (2 John vs.1,2). Did you observe the extraordinary contrast between the two letters where the apostle refers to 'truth'? When addressing Gnostics and all the sons of Adam (1John 1:8) who had not become believers, he places himself in their shoes and emphatically declares: *"If we say that we have no sin, we deceive ourselves, and THE TRUTH IS NOT IN US".* When he singles out and addresses BELIEVERS ONLY in his second epistle he categorically states that the truth *"DWELLETH IN US, AND SHALL BE WITH US FOREVER"* (2John v.2).

Now note another remarkable contrast. When we compare each and every New Testament epistle where believers are specifically addressed, an amazing pattern emerges. At the beginning of every letter the Spirit of God led the writers to give a very special greeting. That greeting is exclusive to believers who have become children of God. It cannot apply to anyone who has not received Jesus Christ as Saviour. Here is the greeting: ***"Grace to you and peace from God OUR FATHER and from the Lord Jesus Christ."*** This greeting is found in all the following letters: Romans 1:7; 1Cor.1:3; 2Cor.1:2; Gal.1:3; Eph.1:2; Phil.1:2; Col.1:2; 1Thes.1:1; 2Thes.1:2; 1Tim.1:2; 2Tim.1:2; Titus 1:4; Philemon 1:3; 1Pet.1:2; 2Pet.1:2; Jude v2 and 2John v.3 That blessed greeting is glaringly missing in 1John chapter one. Why? 1John chapter one is not addressed to believers.The Spirit of God would never extend His peace to anyone outside of Christ.

Now note something else that is most significant. In John's second letter that same glorious greeting appears again.(see 2John verse3). Why? As we have already noted, second John is singularly addressed to believers.

That same beautiful greeting appears again in the letter of Jude, but not before he carefully points out that he is writing ***"To them that are sanctified by***

God the Father, and preserved in Jesus Christ, and called" (Jude 1:2).

The truth is a person, Jesus our Lord

Let us further compare the first epistle of John with other scriptures in order that we obey the command to *"rightly divide the Word of Truth"* (2Tim.2:15).

1John 1 verse 8: *"If we* (human creatures) *say that we have no sin, we deceive ourselves* (and could never be saved with that attitude, for Christ 'came not to call the righteous, but sinners to repentance' (Luke 5:32). *and the truth is not in us."* (We have not received Him **who is the truth,** therefore He is not in us and we are not saved. "He that hath the Son hath life, he that hath not the Son hath not life" (1John 5:12). "He dwelleth in us and shall be with us forever" (2John verse2). Since salvation is Christ in the believer, it could never be said of a believer that the truth is not in him as "he that is joined unto the Lord is ONE SPIRIT" (1Cor.6:17) and believers are "hid with Christ in God" (Col 3:3) and **nothing** can separate us. (Rom.8:35-39).

1John Verse 9. (However) *"If we* (human creatures) *confess our sins,* (as the publican did: 'God be merciful to me a sinner') *He is faithful and just to forgive us our sins, and to cleanse us from ALL UNRIGHTEOUSNESS."* (And we go down to our house justified, just like the publican (Luke18:13,14). Those who are justified are clothed with God's righteousness and are called into the fellowship of His Son as were the Corinthians 1Cor. 1:9).   (Note: To read 1John quotes in continuity, read words in italics only.)

When we come to God initially as the publican did, (saying that we have sin), God forgives us for sins of the past, sins of the present and sins of the future - for **all** of our sins were future when Christ our Saviour died. Moreover, His blood *"keeps on cleansing us from all sin"* (1John 1:7) until the very moment we see Him face to face. That is the gospel, and the gospel means 'good news'. Have you confessed (agreed with God that you are a sinner) and accepted that once and for all forgiveness? If you have, there is only one thing left for you to do and that is *"By Him therefore let us offer the sacrifice of praise to God CONTINUALLY, that is, the fruit of our lips giving THANKS to His name"* (Heb.13:15). If we obey that command there is no room left for ongoing confession with asking for repeated forgiveness.

John included himself with sinners

We should take particular notice that in 1John chapter 1, John had the courtesy to include himself when giving instruction to non-believers. We need to repeat again that he placed himself squarely in their shoes. This fact can be very plainly seen in the following verses where he was definitely addressing non-believers:

1. *"If we say that we have fellowship with Him, and walk in darkness, we lie, and do not the truth"* (1John1:6).

   a). John knew very well that he was already delivered from the power of darkness and had been translated into the kingdom of God's dear Son. (Col.1:18).

   b). He knew that he was not lying but was rather rejoicing in the truth. Yet he included himself with the Gnostics and all unbelievers who were indeed lying.

2. *"If we say that we have no sin, we deceive ourselves,* (The Gnostics claimed that they had no sin) *and the truth is not in us"* (1John 1:8).

   a). John himself knew that he could never say that he had no sin because the Spirit of God residing within alerted him to the truth spoken by Paul *"I am carnal, sold unto sin"* (Rom.7:14).

b). John also knew that the truth was indeed in him, as he had opened the door of his life to the one who is the Way, the Truth and the Life. We noted earlier that in his second epistle he specifically addresses the elect lady and her children. The special note of his word again as it is extremely important. *"The elder unto the elect lady and her children, whom I love in the truth; and not I only, but also all they that have known the truth; for the truth's sake, WHICH DWELLETH IN US, AND SHALL BE WITH US FOREVER"* (2John vs:1,2). He also had that glorious promise from the lips of our Saviour that he will abide with us forever. (John 14:16)

3. *"If we confess our sins, He is faithful and just to forgive us our sins, and to cleanse us from all unrighteousness"* (1John 1:9).

a). John was very much aware that he had confessed his sins, as it is the very first step in receiving the Saviour. He also knew that he was forgiven forever, as he used the aorist tense in that verse to express the finality of forgiveness once confession is made.

b). John knew that all believers are forgiven forever the instant they confess that they are sinners and receive the Saviour. He states that truth in positive terms to all who believe: ***"I write unto you, little children, because your sins ARE forgiven you for His name's sake"*** (1John 2:12). Take special notice that he did not state that your sins **WILL BE** forgiven you. Neither did he state that your sins **ARE BEING** forgiven. His statement could not be more emphatic and final: ***"Your sins ARE forgiven you."*** That means sins of the past, sins of the present, and sins of the future. For all our sins were future when our Saviour died on the Cross. (See 1John 3:1-3).

c). John knew that he was continually being cleansed by the blood of Christ as He used the on-going Greek tense in the latter part of verse seven (1John 1:7) to express that truth.

4.***" If we say that we have not sinned, we make Him a liar, and His word is not in us"*** (1John 1:10).

a). John like Paul, would be the first to declare that he sinned. But he placed himself in the shoes of the unbelieving Gnostics who were claiming that they had never done so.

b). John knew that Jesus, the Word of God, was indeed in him. He declared in 1John 5:12: ***"He that hath the Son hath life; and he that hath not the Son of God hath not life"***. In all the above noted verses John includes himself with sinners (Gnostics and others) who were refusing to confess that they were indeed sinners.

Four critical steps to salvation

There are four critical steps taken by the sinner before he is saved. The sinner may be totally unaware that he is taking them. However, the following order is generally followed:

1. He must confess that he is a sinner. The Greek word for 'confession' means to agree with God.

2. He must repent. Repent means to have 180 degree change of mind.

3. He must believe, i.e., place his entire trust in Christ.

4. He must call, *"For whosoever shall call upon the name of the Lord shall be saved"* (Rom.10:13).

It is difficult to put these in a rigid order as they usually occur simultaneously. In the case of the apostle Paul's conversion they occurred after Christ came upon him by supernatural power.

1. Paul, and all Jews for that matter, were accustomed to repeated confession and sacrifice under the old covenant. On the day of atonement

they fasted, they confessed, and they sacrificed.

2. He repented. He counted his former religious activities as refuse that he might win Christ.

3. He believed. He declared, I know whom I have believed and that He is able to keep that which I have committed unto Him against that day.

4. He called, Who art thou Lord? Lord what wilt thou have me to do?

The Word of God records occasions where people came to him at various stages of the steps just mentioned. They were directed according to the stage they were at at the particular time. The thief on the Cross had already gone through three stages before he fulfilled the fourth stage of calling on the name of the Lord.

1. He confessed he was a sinner. He said to the unrepentant thief: *"We receive the due reward of our deeds"* (Luke 23:41).

2. He repented: He railed on Jesus with the other thief at first. Afterwards he repented..

3. He believed on Jesus: *"but this man hath done nothing amiss"* (Luke 23:41).

4. He called on the name of the Lord *"Lord remember me"*.

Take special note that when he called, Jesus did not tell him to confess his sins. He had already done that in Jesus' presence. Our Lord did not tell him he needed to repent. He had already repented when he called on His name. He did not tell him that he needed to believe on His name. It was only too evident that he had fulfilled that stage. He did not tell him that he must call on the name of the Lord. He had just done that. I am sure that the thief did not know at the time that he had fulfilled every stage necessary (probably in seconds) to receive forgiveness forever. Then he heard the most wonderful words that can fall on human ears: *"Today shalt thou be with Me in paradise"* (Luke 23:43).

Next we have the record of Peter's reply to the Jews on the day of Pentecost *"Men and brethren what must we do?"* The answer was **not** to confess their sins; their attitude demonstrated that they had passed that stage. Therefore Peter replied: *"Repent and be baptized every one of you in the name of Jesus Christ for the remission of sins"* (Acts 2:38). Evidently they had not reached the stage of repentance. They needed to turn from trying to establish their own righteousness under the law, and put their trust in Christ who is *"the end of the law for righteousness to everyone that believeth"* (Rom.10:4).

We find another example in the case of the

Phillipian jailer. He cried out *"What must I do to be saved?"* (Acts 16:30). From the message he heard it is evident that he agreed that he was a sinner. He fell trembling at the apostles' feet in repentance. He called out for salvation. There was only one thing left. He needed to be told that he must *"believe on the Lord Jesus Christ, and thou shalt be saved"* (Acts 16:30). Other examples could be given where the Spirit of God directed His servants at the particular stage of their move toward God, but this is sufficient to help us understand why different direction was given to each one.

In 1John 1:9 the ones who were addressed had never come to stage one. The apostle John did not tell them to repent as Peter did to the Jews on the day of Pentecost. He did not tell them that they needed to believe on the Lord Jesus Christ as Paul instructed the jailer. He did not tell them they needed to call upon the name of the Lord in order to be saved as Paul wrote in Romans 10:13. John was addressing, primarily, Gnostics who had to consent to the first stage of coming to God, that is confess, or agree with God, that they were sinners. **No other people in the entire New Testament** were ever told to confess their sins. When we are aware that the Gnostics would not accept the fact that they were sinners we readily see that the necessity of confession was addressed primarily to them in 1John 1:9.

What About The Lord's Prayer?

Many people today are confused about the wording in the prayer our Lord gave His disciples before He fulfilled the law on the cruel Cross. When our Lord gave instructions to His disciples as to how to pray, He was responding to their own request: *"One of His disciples said unto Him, Lord, teach us to pray, as John also taught his disciples"* (Luke 11:1). If we ignore the time frame when the Lord's prayer was given, we will not be obeying His command to rightly divide the word of truth. Furthermore we will be in confusion ourselves and very likely pass on our confusion to others. Jesus came to His own people the Jews (Israel), while they were living under the Law Covenant He had established with them at Mount Sinai. That covenant on God's part could NEVER be broken until it had been totally fulfilled at the Cross.

At Sinai God revealed His awesome presence to all the people in order to indelibly imprint upon them the seriousness and binding nature of that Blood Covenant. When Moses declared the Words of the Law to them, they responded with one voice, *"all that you have spoken we will do"* (Ex.19:8). The mount could not be touched, it burned with fire, there was *"blackness, and darkness, and tempest, and the sound of a trumpet, and the voice of words, which voice they that heard entreated that the word should not be spoken to them any more. For they could not endure that which was commanded, and if so much as a beast touched the mountain, it shall be stoned, or thrust through with a dart. And so terrible was the sight, that Moses said, I exceedingly fear and quake"* (Heb.12:18-21).

The rigid and binding nature of the law can be seen in the words of Jesus when He declared in positive terms *"One jot or one tittle shall in no wise pass from the law till all be fulfilled."* Furthermore, He declared that He did not come to destroy the law but "to fulfill it" (Matt.5:17,18). Fulfill it He did, to the last jot and tittle, when *"by the eternal Spirit He offered Himself without spot to God"* (Heb.9:14), *"and put away sin by the sacrifice of Himself"* (Heb.9:26).

The Law Covenant was ratified by the blood of bulls and goats, which blood was sprinkled in the presence of God upon all the people. The people with one consent agreed that they would keep their part of the bargain. Three times they cried out *"all that thou hast spoken we will do"* (Ex.19:8; 24:3,7). *"For when Moses had spoken every precept to all the people according to the law, he took the blood of calves and of goats, with water, and scarlet wool, and hyssop, and sprinkled both the book, and all the people, saying, this is the blood of the [covenant] which God has enjoined unto you"* (Heb.9:19,20).

It is most obvious that those who desire to be under the old Law Covenant are placing themselves under the blood of animals *"which can never take away sins"* (Heb.10:11). Those who receive Christ are in a totally New Covenant relationship that He ratified with His own blood when He *"put away sin by the sacrifice of Himself"* (Heb.9:26). Our blessed Saviour now stands in our place with wounded hands and feet and with a riven side. When God establishes a covenant with man, He never deviates from that covenant. Man may chisel and try to sidestep his part, but it should go without saying that God never will. The Law Covenant remained in full force until it was completely fulfilled by the violent death of Christ on the terrible Cross.

When Jesus therefore gave what is commonly called the Lord's prayer to His disciples, not one jot or tittle of the law was overlooked. Unless we keep that fact in mind, the New Covenant promises of total once-for-all forgiveness, with no performance on our part, are a glaring contradiction. The prayer He gave them had to be in perfect keeping with the covenant agreed upon at Mount Sinai. He declared very plainly: *"I am not sent but unto the lost sheep of the house of Israel"* (Matt.15:24). He also forbade His disciples to go outside the confines of the house of Israel: *"These twelve Jesus sent forth, and commanded them, saying, go not into the way of the Gentiles, and into any city of the Samaritans enter ye not: but go rather to the lost sheep of the house is Israel"* (Matt.10:5,6). The gospel of the Kingdom was **exclusively** to those who were under the Sinaitic Covenant. The Lord's prayer was also exclusively to the ones who alone were under that Law Covenant. The outstanding condition of that covenant was clear and plain: **"IF YE WILL"** (Exodus 19:5). They had to do their part, to which they agreed with one voice *"And all the people answered together, and said, all that the Lord hath spoken we will do. And Moses returned the words of the people unto the Lord"* (Exodus 19:8). We would hasten to add however, that the Lord's prayer, as all Scripture, *"is given by inspiration of God, and is profitable for doctrine, for reproof, for correction, for instruction in righteousness: that the man of God may be perfect, throughly furnished unto all good works"* (2Tim.3:16,17). However, we need to be alert and sensitive to the Spirit's direction. He plainly declares that we are to rightly divide the word of truth (2Tim.2:15).

Do not miss the perfect harmony of the Lord's

prayer with the rigid terms of the Sinaitic Covenant which was in full force until the death of Christ: *"Forgive us our debts AS WE FORGIVE our debtors"* (Matt.6:12). He went on to say, *"For IF YE forgive men their trespasses, your heavenly Father will also forgive you: but IF YOU FORGIVE NOT men their trespasses, neither will your Father forgive your trespasses"* (vs.14,15).

If we do not clearly see that the Lord's prayer was a prayer given to a people living under the old Law Covenant, (which covenant was fulfilled and abolished, 2Cor.3:13) directions given to us under the **NEW** Covenant will be utterly confusing. Our Lord's words to His disciples who were under the Old Covenant at that time were plainly stated: If you forgive men their debts you will be forgiven. If you forgive not men their trespasses, neither will your heavenly Father forgive your trespasses. What a contrast we find in the New Covenant where God declares: *"I will put my laws into their hearts, and in their minds will I write them; and their sins and iniquities will I remember no more. Now where [forgiveness] of these is, there is no more offering for sin"* (Heb.10:16-18).

Under the New Covenant of grace the **"if you will"** is completely gone forever. Our forgiveness is now based on the finished work of Christ on the cruel Cross. Because of His eternal sacrifice on the Cross, every believer is now forgiven once and for all and forever. *"I write unto you, little children, because your sins are forgiven you for His name's sake"* (1John 2:12). The preceding promise strictly applies to believers under the New Covenant and will resound throughout all eternity. There are no conditions to be met on the believer's part. The work on the Cross has *"perfected forever them that are sanctified"* (Heb.10:14).

Other New Covenant scriptures reveal the same grand harmonious truths: *"All that believe are justified from all things, from which ye could not be justified by the law of Moses"* (Acts 13:39); *"In whom we have redemption through His blood, the forgiveness of sins, according to the riches of His grace"* (Eph.1:7); *"...forgiving one another, even as God for Christ's sake hath forgiven you"* (Eph. 4:32). Every God-given (New Covenant) promise of instant and total forgiveness is based entirely on the finished work of Christ on the Cross, never on the works of man.

Since the Lord's prayer is often sorted out, elevated and observed above other instruction given by Jesus to a people who were still under the Old Covenant, we need to elaborate on it further by the following points:

1. It was given at the request of the apostles who wanted to pray as did the disciples of John the Baptist (Luke 11:1). The disciples of John (together with the whole nation of Israel) were all under a blood covenant with God that was established at mount Sinai. That covenant was based of the rigid condition "if ye will".

2. The prayer was given by our Lord to the offspring of Israel, the only people **on earth** who were in a special covenant law relationship with Him at that time.

3. The Lord's prayer had to be in perfect keeping with the covenant He had with them at Sinai. He Himself stated that *"one jot or one tittle shall in no wise pass from the law, until all be fulfilled"*(Matt.5:18). The Law Covenant had to be rigidly adhered to. Its terms are built into the Lord's prayer: *"Forgive us our debts, as we forgive our debtors"* (Matt.6:12). The Lord's prayer was followed up immediately by the following words that are also in perfect accord with the Law Covenant: *"For if ye forgive men their trespasses, your heavenly Father will also forgive you: but if ye forgive not men their trespasses, neither will your Father forgive your trespasses"* (Matt.6:14,15). It is not surprising that the outstanding demand of the

Old Covenant is plainly seen in the above words of Jesus: **"if ye will"** (Exodus 19:5). **When our Lord gave the disciples the prayer in question, He abode rigidly with the Old Covenant. That Covenant was still in effect, and had to be adhered to until He Himself totally fulfilled it at the Cross.**

4. a) Jesus Messiah fulfilled the law to the last jot and tittle, by His eternal once-for-all sacrifice on the Cross. b) His death instituted a brand new Blood Covenant. This time, not for Israel alone, but for the whole world. At the last supper He declared: *"This is My blood of the New [Covenant], which is shed for many for the [forgiveness] of sins"* (Matt.26:28). John the Baptist declared of Him: *"Behold the Lamb of God, which taketh away the sin of the world"* (John 1:29).

5. The Old Covenant was established by an agreement of consent with the sons of Jacob (Israel). Its outstanding requirement on the part of the people was: *"If ye will"*. The New Covenant on the other hand was established by God alone who declared: *"I will,"* and repeated it three times in one verse alone (Heb.8:10) in case we might miss the finality of it. There is no *"if ye will"* in the New Covenant. The Scriptures

state *"To him that worketh not, but believeth on Him that justifieth the Ungodly, his faith is counted for righteousness"* (Rom.4:5). The glorious promise of God that **HE WILL** can be seen in every promise that is revealed in the New Covenant. Here is a sample: *"Grace and peace be multiplied unto you through the knowledge of God, and of Jesus our Lord, according as His divine power hath given unto us all things that pertain unto life and godliness, through the knowledge of Him that hath called us to glory and virtue"* (2 Pet.1:2,3). We do not need anything beyond that. That marvelous revelation, in 2 Peter, is another demonstration of God fulfilling His promise of *"I will"* (Heb. 8:10) under the New Covenant.

An incredible contradiction

The greatest contradiction imaginable is seen when believers commemorate the Lord's supper while at the same time they refuse to come out from under the terms of the **Old Covenant.** It is all the more ridiculous when we consider that the Old Covenant had **nothing to do with Gentiles.** Psalm 147:19,20 plainly states: *"He showeth His word unto Jacob, His statutes and His [ordinances] unto Israel. He hath not dealt so with any nation: and as*

for His [ordinances], they have not known them."
We read in Ephesians 2:12 that Gentiles were
*"aliens from the commonwealth of Israel, and
strangers from the covenants of promise."* We
should always bear in mind that our dear Lord
completely fulfilled the Old Covenant by His
violent death at the Cross. *"Christ is the end*
(termination) *of the law for righteousness to every
one that believeth"* (Rom.10:4). For *"the just shall
live by faith and the law is not of faith"* (Gal.
3:11,12).

Our Lord wants us to remember His death until He
returns by symbolically drinking His blood of the
NEW COVENANT, and living thereafter in the
liberty and freedom of it. For *"of Him, and through
Him, and to Him, are all things: to whom be glory
for ever"* (Rom.11:36). At the last supper He
declared: *"this is my blood of the New [Covenant],
which is shed for many for the [forgiveness] of
sins"* (Matt 26:28). Oh how it must grieve our dear
Lord when believers, like the Galatians of old, insist
on living under the terms of the old Law Covenant
that was ratified by the blood of bulls and of goats.

The chosen apostle was led by the Spirit to
confront the Galatians with words of truth that
would set them free from the law: *"Tell me, ye that
desire to be under the law,* (there are still those who

desire to be under the law) *do ye not hear the law? For it is written that Abraham had two sons, the one by a bondmaid, the other by a freewoman. But he who was of the bondwoman was born after the flesh; but he of the free woman was by promise. which things are an allegory: for these are the two covenants;* (law and grace) *the one from the Mount Sinai, which gendereth to bondage, which is Agar. For this Agar is Mount Sinai in Arabia, and answereth to Jerusalem which now is, and is in bondage with her children. But Jerusalem which is above is free, which is the mother of us all...Now we, brethren, as Isaac was, are the children of promise. But as then he that was born after the flesh persecuted him that was born after the Spirit, even so it is now. Nevertheless what sayeth the Scripture? Cast out the bondwoman and her son: for the son of the bondwoman shall not be heir with the son of the free woman. So then, brethren, we are not children of the bondwoman, but of the free. Stand fast therefore in the liberty wherewith Christ has made us free, and be not entangled again with the yoke of bondage"* (Gal. 4:21-5:1).

Could our loving God make it any plainer? These are the two covenants. All that was given at Sinai was transitory, and had to go when it was fulfilled at the Cross. Law and grace cannot mix. It must be one or the other. *"The just shall live by faith. And the law is not of faith"* (Gal. 3:11,12). *"And if by grace, then is it no more of works: otherwise grace is no more grace. But if it be of works: then is it no more grace: otherwise work is no more work"* (Rom.11:6). Sad to say there are a great many today who will not obey the Spirit's command to cast out the bondwoman and her son. As a result they ever remain in spiritual bondage. The liberating truth given to the Spirit-instructed apostle can do nothing for them as long as they refuse to receive it. He declared, and it is written: *"For through the law I died to the law, that I might live to God. I have been crucified with Christ; and it is no longer I who live, but Christ lives in me; and the life which I now live in the flesh I live by faith in the Son of God, who loved me, and delivered Himself up for me. I do not nullify the grace of God; for if righteousness comes through the law, then Christ died needlessly"* (Gal.2:19-21, NAS).This should be the settled testimony of every believer. However, it is sad to say that those who *"desire to be under the law"* can never, in truth, join the apostle in that marvelous proclamation. If they have not cast out the bondwoman and her son they are merely voicing meaningless words.

CHAPTER 6

Giving thanks always results in the joy of the Lord

All that God desires of us now, **as forgiven and constantly being cleansed sinners,** is to continually thank Him profusely for what He has done on our behalf. Note what He says to all believers: *"Let the peace of God rule in your hearts,...and be ye THANKFUL" "and whatsoever ye do in word or deed, do all in the name of the Lord Jesus, GIVING THANKS"* (Col.3:15,17). *"Be filled with the Spirit...GIVING THANKS ALWAYS FOR ALL THINGS unto God and the Father in the name of our Lord Jesus Christ"* (Eph.5:18,20). *"By Him therefore let us offer the sacrifice of praise to God CONTINUALLY, that is, the fruit of our lips GIVING THANKS TO HIS NAME"* (Heb.13:15). When we live with an attitude of constant thankfulness to God for all that He has done, is doing, and will do for us throughout all eternity, we will understand what He means by His command to us to *"Rejoice evermore"* (1Thes.5:16); *"Rejoice in the Lord always; and again I say, rejoice"* Phil.4:4.

Confession of sin is the initial act of the sinner

When we take into account the above noted Scriptures it should be obvious that 1John 1:9 is for the sinner who, like the publican, repents for the **first time.** He is then instantly forgiven and goes back to his house justified - just as if he had never sinned. Jesus said of the publican: *"This man went down to his house justified"* (Luke 18:14). As a matter of fact there are 33 recorded things God does for the sinner the moment he receives Christ as Saviour. The following are a few: He is instantly forgiven and called into the fellowship of His Son Jesus Christ our Lord (1Cor.1:9). He is translated out of the kingdom of darkness into the kingdom of God's dear Son (Col.1:13). He is sealed with the Holy Spirit until the day of redemption (Eph. 1:13,14). He is kept by the power of God from falling and will be presented faultless before God's Holy throne (Jude 24).

We should always be aware of the revealed fact that a sinner is totally saved the instant he receives the Saviour. God clothes him with His righteousness. Even if he lived to be a hundred and never sinned again he would be no more fit for heaven than he was the instant he received the Saviour. The Word of God declares that every sinner who comes to God in repentance instantly receives

"Abundance of grace and of the gift of righteousness" (Rom.5:17).

There is a common desire in all of us to work everything out for ourselves. Along with that desire is the notion that we are capable of doing it. That notion is deadly when we carry it into the realm of salvation from sin. God was referring to this trait when He referred to religious Israel. *"For they being ignorant of God's righteousness, and going about to establish their own righteousness, have not submitted themselves unto the righteousness of God"* (Rom.10:3). Ongoing confession and asking for forgiveness helps to satisfy our desire to play a role in our own deliverance. If indeed there was a role fallen man could play, be it ever so small, our righteous God would have to credit him for it. In the perfect economy of God, glory would have to be given where it is due. However, there is only one worthy of credit because He paid it all. To Him be glory both now and forever, for *"He is able also to save them to the uttermost them that come unto God by Him, seeing He ever liveth to make intercession for them"* (Heb.7:25).

Further proof that 1John 1:9 refers to ones outside of Christ is found in 1John 1:4, Amp: *"We are now writing these things to you so that our joy [in seeing you included] may be full - and your joy may be complete."* Do not miss this declaration. The apostle clearly indicates that he is addressing individuals who are not included in the household of faith. He points out to them that when they confess that they are indeed sinners and receive the Saviour, his joy will be full and so will theirs. This translation, in the amplified version, is true to the original Greek text.

Justification of sin a truth often ignored

"Those whom God has called unto salvation He justified, that is, He takes away the guilt and penalty of their sins and bestows upon them a positive righteousness, even Jesus Christ Himself in whom the believer stands forever innocent, uncondemned, and righteous in point of law." (Romans 8:30), Wuest's Word Studies. 1

Surely the one who is now forever innocent, uncondemned and righteous need never go back again to confess and ask for forgiveness. To do so would demonstrate that he or she never accepted God's truth in Rom.8:30. The forever forgiven sinner needs only to **thank God for Calvary** every time he sees sin raise its ugly head.

The forgiven justified sinner is never told to confess (why would he need to confess if already forgiven and justified?) or try to fight or overcome sin. He is rather instructed to *"walk in the Spirit"* in order that he not fulfill the lust of the flesh (Gal.5:16).

We should take special note again that God's word to the redeemed and justified sinner is not to confess his sins, but rather to *"put off all these; anger, wrath, malice, blasphemy, filthy communication out of your mouth ...and put on therefore, as the elect of God, HOLY and BELOVED* (Since God addresses His children as elect, holy, and beloved, why would those who are made holy by God confess their sins? There could be only one reason - they refuse to believe God's infallible Word that He has made them holy in Christ Jesus and has 'perfected forever them that are sanctified' (Heb.10:14.) *[tender] mercies, kindness, humbleness of mind, meekness, long suffering, forbearing one another, and forgiving one another,... EVEN AS CHRIST FORGAVE YOU"* (Col.3:8,12,13). (Note: To read Col. quote in continuity, read words in italics only.)

God's marvelous basis for forgiving others

God commands us to forgive others because He has forgiven us (Col.3:13). This is in vast contrast to the Old Covenant. It is also another great demonstration of God fulfilling His promise of *"I will"* (Heb.8:10) under the New Covenant. He bases our forgiving others on the fact that He has already forgiven us (see Eph.4:32). If we insist on repeated confession, asking for forgiveness, we destroy God's basis for our need to forgive others. If we are not forgiven now and forever, the command has no force and is therefore meaningless. Stop and meditate on that fact, and rejoice in God's great New Covenant basis for our forgiving of others who offend us.

The wonderful harmony of God's established truth

When we recognize that 1John 1:9 is for the sinner coming to God for the first time, a flood of Scriptures fall into harmony. The apostle John in 1John 2:1 singles out those who came to God in accord with 1John 1:9. He addresses them as *"my little children"*. He proceeds to answer the great question: "if a born again believer sins, what then?" False notions respecting this critical area of the believer's life have kept millions of humble believers in bondage down through the centuries. Let every mouth be stopped, and let every notion of man be silenced. Let doctrines of demons be throttled for ever and let us bow before the great

Word of God. Let us now hear the Word of God alone: *"My little children, if anyone sins"* If you are a child of God He is speaking directly to you. Listen!!! Does He declare that we make a move and immediately confess? No! A THOUSAND TIMES NO. That is the traditional notion of men that makes the Word of God of no effect (Mark 7:13). Shut out false notions and hear Him alone: *"we have an advocate (lawyer) with the Father, Jesus Christ the righteous one."* (1John 2:1) Marvel of marvels, wonder of wonders. When we sin as God's children, our God informs us here that **we do not make the move, He does,** as He did for Peter hours before Peter sinned. OUR ALL WISE GLORIOUS SAVIOUR AND HEAD OF THE BODY HANDLES IT FOR US, BECAUSE HE LOVES US AND HAS DIED FOR EVERY SIN WE HAVE COMMITTED OR EVER WILL COMMIT WHILE WE ARE IN THIS FRAIL HUMAN BODY.

Every time we sin as believers, our advocate is on the scene in the same instant, (or perhaps even in eternity past?) interceding on our behalf. Behold the prints of the nails in His hands, and His wounded side. *"He died for our sins, was buried, and rose again the third day"* (1Cor.15:3,4). *"Who shall lay anything to the charge of God's elect?* (Do we sin? Yes!) *It is God that justifieth. Who is he that condemneth? It is Christ that died, yea rather, that is risen again, who is even on the right hand of God, who also maketh intercession for us"* (Romans 8:33,34).

We never know how dreadfully we sin according to God's estimation of sin, but He has already taken care of all sins at the old rugged Cross where He suffered, bled and died in our place. When I know I fail him miserably, I can only come with a heart of profound thanksgiving for all that He did and is doing on my behalf. He recognizes and takes care of my miserable failures long before they come to the forefront of my poor finite mind. How comforting and how wonderful to know that *"He is able also to save them to the UTTERMOST that come unto God by Him, seeing He ever liveth to make intercession for them"* (Heb.7:25).

Note the continued harmony of the Word as the apostle John specifically continues to address God's children: *"Your sins ARE forgiven you for His name's sake"* (1John 2:12). That has to include past, present and future sins of the believer. If it did not include sins of the future, that particular promise would be invalid by the time it reached the believers to whom it was first addressed. Why? Because they sinned while the letter was in transit.

Believers are perfected forever
by the work of the Cross

In 1Cor.6:11, the believer is informed that *"ye are washed, ye are sanctified, ye are justified"*. In Hebrews, the believer is told, *"By one offering HE HATH PERFECTED FOREVER them that are sanctified"* (Heb.10:14). If we keep running back to God confessing our sins, are we not, in effect, robbing Hebrews 10:14 of its meaning? Are we not also demonstrating that we do not believe a word of it? If 1John 1:9 is for the believer, how could those Scriptures harmonize? Those whom God has perfected **forever** surely need never go back to the Lord in confession asking for forgiveness. The Cross and the ongoing cleansing takes care of that. The ones whom He has perfected forever need only to go on thanking Him that He *"put away sin by the sacrifice of Himself"* (Heb.9:26). When the Spirit of God is allowed to refresh these great truths to our hearts, the following words of our Saviour in John's gospel become ever more precious: *"He that heareth my word, and believeth on Him that sent me, HATH EVERLASTING LIFE, and shall not come into condemnation; but IS passed from death unto life"* (John 5:24).

CHAPTER 7

Believers to count on the fact of their death with Christ

In Romans chapters five to seven, the Word of God goes into lengthy details regarding the whole sin question since the fall of Adam. The responsibility of the Christian respecting sin is thoroughly covered in every detail, but never once does the apostle give instruction to the born-again Christian to confess sins to God. His teaching is to the contrary. ***"Likewise reckon*** (count on the fact) ***ye also yourselves to be dead indeed unto sin, but alive unto God through Jesus Christ our Lord"*** (Rom.6:11). William R. Newell comments on this verse as follows: *"We are not told to die to sin: because we are in Christ who did die to it; and therefore we also are DEAD to it, in His death; and reckon it so. This should make the believer's task simplicity itself. The only difficulty lies in BELIEVING these astounding revelations! That we should be dead to sin, and now alive unto God as risen ones, sharing that newness of life (verse 4) which our Lord began as "the first-born from among the dead," is at first too wonderful for us. We see in ourselves the old self-life, the flesh - and straightway we forget God's way of faith, and turn back to our 'feelings'. We say, 'Alas, if I could* *escape from this body, I would be free'. But that is not at present God's plan for you and me. We WAIT for the redemption of our body. This body is yet unredeemed. Nevertheless, we are to RECKON ourselves dead unto sin and alive unto God. Not dead to sin, notice, through prayers and strugglings, nor dead to sin in our feelings or consciousness; but IN THAT DEATH UNTO SIN WHICH CHRIST WENT THROUGH ON THE CROSS, and which we SHARED, and IN THAT LIFE which He now lives in glory!*

"It has pleased God to call for our faith, both in connection with salvation and with deliverance. Therefore, if we would obey and please God, let us follow His methods! Let us learn to RECKON OURSELVES DEAD - that Christ's death to sin was our death; and is the present relation of us who are IN Christ, unto sin. The path of faith is always against appearances, - or, if you will, against human consciousness. God says certain things; and we, obeying the 'law of faith', say the same things, like Abraham, not regarding our own body, which says the contrary thing. (The record of Abraham's attitude [Rom.4:19] is a marvelous illustration for us. Do not miss it.)   *Facts are facts; and these are what God reveals to us. Appearances, or 'feelings' are a wholly different thing from facts! God says, 'You died to sin: reckon yourself dead!' Obedient*

souls do so, and enter the path of deliverance in experience. Doubting souls fall back on their 'feelings,' and turn back to prayers (of confession) *and struggles, avoiding FAITH."* 1 (Note: Comments in brackets are mine.)

Believers to count themselves dead to sin and alive to God

Every time we come to God confessing our sins as born-again believers we are, in effect, demonstrating that we will not obey His command to *"reckon ye also yourselves to be dead indeed unto sin, but alive unto God through Jesus Christ our Lord"* (Rom.6:11). Those who insist on a continued confession to God, consider themselves very much alive to sin. It cannot be otherwise, unless we twist and distort the straightforward language of the Holy Spirit. I would strongly suggest that we meditate long upon Romans 6:11. It is an enormously strong pill for the flesh to swallow, because it involves its death. Paul himself expressed the same truth in Gal.2:19,20, NAS: *"For through the law I died to the Law, that I might live to God. I have been crucified with Christ, and it is no longer I who live, but Christ lives in me, and the life which I now live in the flesh I live by faith in the Son of God, who loved me, and delivered*

Himself up for me". Paul reckoned himself dead indeed unto sin, but alive unto God through Jesus Christ our Lord. What was true of Paul is true of every born-again believer with no exceptions whatsoever. That is why Paul never taught believers to confess their sins to God. That teaching, so widespread today, nullifies the great liberating truths of Romans chapter 6, Col.3:3,4, etc. Oh, how we need to lay hold on the glorious truth that is forever settled in heaven, *"ye are dead, and your life is hid with Christ in God. When Christ, who is our life, shall appear, then shall ye also appear with Him in glory"* (Col.3:3,4). Oh, that we would take God at His word, and be constantly aware that His truth abideth for ever.

Believers counted righteous through death with Christ

Take special note of another Spirit-breathed revelation from Romans 6:7, RV: *"For he that hath died* (with Christ Col.3:3,4) *hath been declared righteous* (or freed) *from sin".* W.R.Newell comments: *"We must seize fast hold on this verse. Let us distinguish at once between being justified from sins - from the guilt thereof - by the blood of Christ, and being justified from sin - the thing itself. 'Justified from sin' is the key to both chapters six, seven and eight! It is the consciousness of being sinful that keeps saints back from the glorious life Paul lived.* (Take special note of that statement) *Paul shows absolutely no sense of bondage before God; but goes on in blessed triumph! Why? He knows that he has been justified from all guilt by the blood of Christ; and he knew that he was also justified, cleared, from the thing sin itself; and therefore (though walking in an, as yet, unredeemed body), he was wholly heavenly in his standing, life and relations with God! He knew he was as really justified from sin itself as from sins. The conscious presence of sin in his flesh only reminded him that he was in Christ; - that sin had been condemned judicially, as connected with flesh, at the cross; and that he was justified as to sin, because he had died with Christ, and his former relationship to sin had wholly ceased! Its presence gave him no thought of condemnation, but only eagered his longing for the redemption body. 'Justified from sin' - because, 'he that hath died is justified from sin.' Glorious fact! May we have faith to enter into it as did Paul.*

"*It is the deep-seated notion of Christendom that gradually we become saints, - gradually worthy of heaven, so that sometime, - perhaps on a dying bed, we will have the right to 'drop this robe of flesh and rise.' But Scripture cuts this idea off at once, by the declaration that we died, and that we are now, here, justified from sin! 'Giving thanks to the Father, who made us meet to be partakers of the inheritance of the saints in light.' The saints in light are those in glory, and they are there for one reason alone; the work of Christ on the Cross. How unspeakably sad our little faith! And I am speaking of true believers, certainly."* 2   (Note: comments in brackets are mine.)

The Scriptures are always consistent; they never speak in riddles

It is most obvious why Paul **never** taught born-again believers to confess their sins. He, by the Spirit, revealed the glorious truth that one is *instantly justified* the moment one trusts Christ. If Paul taught believers to confess sins, he would be talking riddles. To teach justification on the one hand and the need for confession on the other hand would be sheer nonsense. K.S. Wuest, an eminent Greek scholar, states the following: *"Justification in the Bible sense is the act of God removing from the believing sinner, his guilt and the penalty incurred by that guilt, and bestowing a positive righteousness, Christ Jesus Himself in whom the believer stands, not only innocent and uncondemned, but actually righteous in point of law for time and for eternity."* 3

Hear this word from the notable Bible teacher of days gone by, H.A.Ironsides. We quote: *"Peter is never said to have preached justification, but forgiveness and remission. Paul adds justification. When God forgives through the risen, glorified Jesus, He not only forgives but He justifies. It is impossible for an earthly judge to both forgive and to justify a man. If a man is justified, he does not need to be forgiven.*(Take special note of that.) *Imagine a man charged with a crime going into court, and after the evidence is all in he is pronounced not guilty and the judge sets him free. Someone says as he leaves the building, 'I want to congratulate you: it was very nice of the judge to forgive you.' 'Forgive nothing! He did not forgive me; I am justified. There is nothing to forgive.'* 4 (Note: comment in brackets is mine.)

God sees all believers clothed in Christ

Those who totally accept God's infallible Word that He justifies the ungodly (Rom.4:5), accounting them righteous by simply believing, could never go back to Him confessing their sins and asking for forgiveness. They should rather **thank Him profusely** for the great and glorious fact of their justification.

In 1John 4:17, we have a marvelous revelation given to us: *"As He is, so are we in this world."* If we believe that great truth, how could we go on confessing sins that were paid for at Calvary? We are as He is because He *"put away sin by the sacrifice of Himself"* (Heb.9:26). He is now in us and we are in Him. *"But by His doing you are in Christ Jesus, who became to us wisdom from God, and righteousness and sanctification, and redemption"* (1Cor.1:30, NAS). If we, as forgiven sinners, go to God confessing our sins, God would have every cause to say *"what sins"*? Do you not believe My word that *"you are washed, you are sanctified, you are justified in the name of the Lord Jesus, and by the Spirit of God"?* (1Cor.6:11). Do you not believe that my Son hath appeared to *"put away sin by the sacrifice of Himself"?* Do you not believe that you have been delivered *"from the power of darkness, and [have been] translated into the kingdom of [my] dear Son, in whom [you] have redemption through His blood, even the forgiveness of sins"?* (Col.1:13,14). Did you not believe Me when I declared: *"their sins and [their lawless acts] will I remember no more"?* (Heb.10:17). Do you not believe My word in Ephesians that you are to *"forgive one another even as God for Christ's sake HAS FORGIVEN you"?* (Eph. 4:32). Are you refusing to believe My Word that you **are forgiven** forever? You are told again and again in My word that you are forgiven, cleansed and made holy. Why don't you rather accept my eternal truth and thank Me for giving you *"abundance of grace and of the gift of righteousness"?* (Rom.5:17).

When we have a proper understanding of the aforementioned Scriptures, we will readily see why the apostle Paul never once gave any instruction regarding confession of sins. Confession of sins, with a request for God to forgive, is foreign to the teaching of the apostle. If we teach God's people to confess their sins for forgiveness when they are assured over and over again in the Word of God that they are already forgiven, are we not encouraging them to live in unbelief? That is a very, very serious fact to consider.

CHAPTER 8

Believers to live in keeping with their high and holy calling

It is most significant that everywhere in the New Testament, where believers were living like the world, the inspired writers **never** instructed them to confess their sins. But note this - they rather remind them of their lofty position in Christ Jesus our Lord. Here are some examples: The apostle Paul declared *"Shall we continue in sin that grace may abound? God forbid"* (Rom.6:1,2). Instead of instructing them to confess their sins, He reveals some of the greatest truths found in the word. *"Ye are dead to sin." "You have been baptized into Jesus Christ." "You were buried with Him." "You were raised with Him." "Yield yourselves therefore unto God." "Sin shall not have dominion over you,"* etc. (Rom.6:3,4,13,14). In view of the above referenced scriptures, would we not have to try to resurrect our sins in order to confess them? Do we sin as Christians? Yes. Did Christ pay the penalty for them? Yes. Does His blood keep on cleansing us? Yes. What more is necessary? Nothing. That is why our Lord never once taught New Covenant believers to confess their sins. Moreover, we may research in every letter written specifically to the churches in the New Testament and never find a word respecting the need of confession on the part of the believer.

The apostle Paul never once instructed carnal Corinthians, or the foolish Galatians, to confess their sins. If any believers needed to run to God in confession, they certainly did, as their sins were varied and many. As an answer to their strife and division, he did not command them to get on their knees before God in confession, but of all things he rather declared: *"We are labourers together with God: ye are God's [cultivated field]"* (1Cor.3:9).

To the ones taking their brethren to law before judges who were unbelievers, he did not command them to go to God in confession, but rather revealed to them that they will one day *"judge the world"* and again, *"Know ye not that we shall judge angels?"* (1Cor.6:2,3).

The believer the dwelling place of God

This was referred to earlier but it bears repeating. To the Corinthians who were practicing the heathen custom of going in to harlots, he never once stated that confession to God must be made immediately, but rather revealed the infallible truth that *"He that is joined unto the Lord is one spirit"* and *"Know ye not that your body is the temple of the Holy Spirit?"* (1Cor.6:17,19). There is only one possible way we as believers can be holy in our walk. That one and only way is by yielding the members of our body to the Holy one who lives within us by His Spirit (Romans 6:13). He who alone is Holy (Rev.15:4) will then manifest His holiness through our yielded members. *"For we who live are constantly being delivered over to death for Jesus' sake, that the life of Jesus also may be manifested in our mortal flesh"* (2Cor.4:11NASB) Any attempt at holiness on our own is an exercise in futility. This fact should destroy every false notion that there is a fleshly performance required on our part. The apostle Paul understood and revealed this great truth by the Spirit when he declared: *"I am carnal, sold under sin. For that which I do I allow not: for what I would, that do I not; but what I hate, that do I...Now then it is no more I that do it, but sin that dwelleth in me...O wretched man that I am! Who shall deliver me from the body of this death? I thank God through Jesus Christ our Lord"* (Rom.7:14-25). When we come to the Saviour in total surrender of heart, having *"no confidence in the flesh"*(Phil.3:3), we experience the glorious deliverance of Christ that was spoken of by the apostle. We will also be granted a perfect understanding of His words of truth in John 6:63: *"it is the SPIRIT that [giveth life], the flesh profiteth nothing."*

Our loving God lays bare His heart, as it were, and discloses what His great longing and desire is for every one of His blood-purchased people. This prayer is Spirit breathed: *"For this reason I bow my knees before the Father,...that He would grant you, according to the riches of His glory to be strengthened with power through His Spirit in the inner man; so that Christ may dwell in your hearts through faith; and that you, being rooted and grounded in love, may be able to comprehend with all the saints what is the breadth and length and height and depth, and to know the love of Christ which surpasses knowledge, THAT YOU MAY BE FILLED UP TO ALL THE FULLNESS OF GOD. Now to Him that is able to do exceeding abundantly beyond all that we ask or think, according to the power that works within us, to Him be glory in the church and in Christ Jesus to all generations for ever and ever"* (Eph.3:14-21, NAS).

There are five amazing desires of God expressed in that prayer. They encompass everything God longs for on behalf of all believers, otherwise more than five would be included. Carefully note that confession of sins and activity on the part of the flesh is glaringly absent. Here are God's great desires simply stated:

1. That we might be strengthened with power by His Spirit in the inner man.

2. That Christ may settle down, and make His home in our hearts through faith, or that He may by our consent take over and occupy every area of our personality.

3. That we may know the love of Christ which is infinitely beyond our comprehension.

4. That we might be rooted and grounded in love, so that our whole life bears the fruit of love that flows through the vine who is Jesus Christ our Lord (John 15:5).

5. That we may be filled with all the fullness of God, our whole life being a manifestation of the fruit of the Spirit (Gal.5:22,23).

The above list comprehends God's ultimate desire for every child of His. God desires nothing more than the five points found in that prayer, but nothing less will satisfy Him.

Oh, how different (from ours) are God's ultimate desires, as expressed in that prayer in Ephesians chapter 3.

1. When we are filled with all the fullness of God, the world will see God's behaviour, not our's, and the fruit of the Spirit will be manifest to every one we come in contact with. We will be

operating in the strength of Almighty God who created heaven and earth and all that in them is.

2. When we are filled with all the fullness of God we will cease trying to do our best for Jesus, but like the apostle Paul our testimony will always be: *"I have been crucified with Christ; and it is no longer I that live, but Christ lives in me"* (Galatians 2:20, NAS).

3. If we are filled with all the fullness of God, it could never be us working for God, but rather God at work in us *"both to will and to do of His good pleasure"* (Phil.2:13).

4. If we are filled with all the fullness of God, the one who alone knows where to seek and to save the lost ones will lead us to the very doorstep of seeking hearts who have already been wooed by the Holy Spirit. It will save an incredible amount of time and self effort. It will also avoid infuriating individuals whose hearts have not been prepared beforehand by the Holy Spirit. Remember God's direction to Paul and Silas. They were *"Forbidden by the Holy Spirit to speak the Word in Asia; and when they had come to Mysia, they were trying to go into Bithynia, and the Spirit of Jesus did not permit them"* (Acts16:6,7, NAS). Both Asia and Bythinia had been locked in heathen darkness

for centuries. Obviously there was an incredible need in both provinces. Nevertheless, they were not a part of God's program at that particular time. When we are dispatched by God on His timetable, He will take our yielded vocal chords that He formed with His own hands and will speak words of life to the dead in trespasses and sins, and they will come alive.

5. If we are filled with all the fullness of God we can never burn out on a mission field, because we will be sent and accompanied by the Almighty God who sent us. He *"upholds all things by the word of His power"* (Heb.1:3). His never failing strength therefore, is inexhaustible.

Filled with all the fullness of God

Our Lord makes it very, very clear that His one great desire for us is that we be filled with all the fullness of Himself. SINCE FULL IS FULL, there is no room left for us to try to do our so-called best for Jesus. It also removes all notions from our minds that we can do anything for God. He does not need anything *"seeing HE GIVETH TO ALL LIFE, and breath, and all things"* (Acts17:25). The believer has been *"crucified with Christ;"* and he no longer lives, but Christ lives in him (Gal.2:20 NAS.) There is really only one missionary, one preacher, one teacher. He is the omnipresent Lord of Glory who lives in every believer by His Spirit. *"Now if any man have not the Spirit of Christ, he is none of His"* (Rom.8:9). Man was never created to function on his own. He was created to be inhabited by Almighty God. Jeremiah spoke an eternal truth when he stated: *"It is not in man that walketh to direct his steps"* (Jer.10:23). With that critical information from the One who created us, may we never be foolish enough to waste time in the attempt, but rather yield our members to the only One who can do the work (Rom. 6:13).

If there was anything that God wanted us to do on our own, without Him, He would leave some room for us to function. However, that Spirit-breathed prayer in Eph. 3 reveals God's ultimate desire for every one of us. It covers everything and proves that He is satisfied with nothing less than total right-of-way in our lives. We see the amazing harmony with this in Rom.6:13 when He asks us to: *"Yield yourselves unto God, as those that are alive from the dead, and your members as instruments of righteousness unto God"*. It cannot be both ways; either we are obeying that command, living in an attitude of total dependance on God, or we are operating in the energy of the flesh, trying to do our best for Him. Our Lord gave us a remarkable revelation on this subject in John 12:26 when He declared a very simple but most profound truth: ***"Where I am there shall also my servant be"***. It is impossible to serve our Lord in His absence. He who is the mighty God of the universe is waiting for our consent to ***"make [us] perfect in every good work to do His will, WORKING IN [US] that which is well pleasing in His sight, through Jesus Christ; to whom be glory for ever and ever"*** (Heb.13:21).

It should thrill our hearts to learn that God expects nothing of us but total failure. He needs no help from any of His created beings. ***"God that made the world and all things therein, seeing that He is Lord of heaven and earth, dwelleth not in temples made with hands; neither is worshipped with men's hands, as though He needed anything, seeing He giveth to all life, and breath, and all things"*** (Acts 17:24,25). Our Lord's Word to us is good news to the maximum. ***"Come unto me, all ye that labour and are heavy laden, and I will give you REST"***. He does not stop there but continues by declaring ***"Take my yoke upon you, and learn of me; for I am meek and lowly in heart: and ye shall find REST unto your souls"*** (Matt.11:28,29). From a human point of view these were strange words spoken by our Saviour, especially when we consider that there was a whole world that He was about to reach with the gospel message. The more we learn of Him, howevcr, the more we discover the ***"greatness of His power to us-ward who believe"*** (Eph.1:19). Instead of us working for Him, we learn that He ***"is able to do exceeding abundantly above all that we ask or think, according to the power that worketh in us"*** (Eph.3:20). He therefore begs us to ***"present [our] bodies a living sacrifice"*** (Rom.12:1) in order that He take over and do all the work through our yielded members. He will not cut across the boundaries of our will. We may go on living in self-imposed poverty, sweating it out for God, and yet accomplishing nothing that counts in the eternal economy of God. On the other hand, we can surrender our all to Him and enter into the glorious rest He is offering. He in turn will fulfill His plans that count for eternity through us, and reward **us** in the future for it. It is wise to meditate very much on the prayer in Ephesians 3:14-21, for it is an amazing revelation of the sum total of what God desires of us.

Steve McVey has an excellent comment on the above truth: *"The victorious Christian life is nothing less than the life of Christ expressed through the life of the child of God. ANY behaviour which is not dependent on Him living His life through us comes from the flesh. That suggests that it is even possible to be busy doing things FOR God while our actions still stem from the energy of the flesh. THE EXCHANGED LIFE MEANS THAT WE*

DEPEND ON HIS RESOURCES, NOT ON OUR OWN. FLESH LIFE MEANS DEPENDING ON WHAT I CAN DO. We may be well respected for our zeal and service to Christ and yet be relying on the flesh. God has no desire to help US to live the Christian life or to do the work of Christian ministry. He wants to do it Himself - THROUGH us. Major Ian Thomas has said:

"There is nothing quite so nauseating or pathetic as the flesh trying to be holy! The flesh has a perverted bent for righteousness - but such righteousness as it may achieve is always self-righteousness; and self-righteousness is always self-conscious righteousness; and self-conscious righteousness is always full of self-praise. This produces the extrovert, who must always be noticed, recognized, consulted, and applauded. On the other hand, when the flesh in pursuit of self-righteousness fails, instead of being filled with self-praise, it is filled with self-pity, and this produces the introvert. A professional "case" for professional counselors!"

"Trying to do something FOR God is a flesh trip! It is possible to be sincere in trying to do something for Him, yet be sincerely wrong. Religious flesh is often a hard pattern for a person to recognize because it is usually applauded by other Christians. Religious service may cause you to be pleased with

yourself. Or it may leave you feeling spiritually and emotionally drained. If you find yourself in either place, God may be trying to show you the problem. Many Christians today are exhausted because they understand the Christian life to be primarily a life of service for God. But that isn't true. The Christian life is primarily a life of intimacy WITH God." 1

The greatest harvest in church history

The greatest demonstration of God's mighty power to save the lost is found in the history of the church. That power was released through believers who were strengthened by His might and filled with all His fullness. Historians record that half the Roman Empire was converted to Christ in the first 200 years of Church history. When we consider the fact that the Church was under the most severe persecution of its history during most of those years, we marvel at the incredible impact it had on the world in that short period of time. Ten Roman emperors inflicted the most cruel and atrocious tortures upon believers known to mankind. They attempted to stamp out the Christian Church completely.

Church leaders could not plan missionary ventures, nor could they launch programs of any kind to evangelize the world. Believers who tried to program for God were soon reported, and their property was taken from them. Most of them were imprisoned and many of them were tortured and fed to wild, starving animals in sport arenas where thousands of spectators saw them torn to pieces and die. Yet never in the history of the world has the gospel reached mankind to the extent that it did in that particular short period of time. It seemed God allowed the terrible persecutions to go on because He knew that those who suffered through it would rely on Him in a way not possible when the Church is more or less accepted in the world.

The greatest program in the history of the world to rescue and release fallen humanity was launched by Almighty God Himself at that time. The forces of darkness holding the bulk of humanity in its deadly grip were aligned to prevent the glorious gospel from reaching a lost world. God's great missionary program for the world had to be planned and programmed by God Himself, alone. He knew that the forces of darkness would quickly frustrate the plans and programs of men. Every move to reach the world was to be accomplished by His action in His body the Church.

Terrible measures had to be taken in order that believers would totally rely on Him at all times. When they did, supernatural strength was given to them to endure some of the most dreadful tortures the world has ever known. They suffered unspeakable torments. Many of them died martyr's deaths with exceeding joy in their hearts, a song of praise to God on their lips, and a heavenly smile on their faces. Their attitude and their words demonstrated to a heathen world the reality of the gospel of God's grace. As a result multiplied thousands turned to the Christ at that time. They saw the Saviour manifested before them in the lives of those who had trusted Him completely. Oh! What eternal rewards await those who suffered and died at the hands of their persecutors. According to *Foxe's Christian Martyrs of the World,* five million believers suffered a martyr's death by the scourge of Rome during that period of time.

CHAPTER 9

Only God's own righteousness can satisfy God

Since the only righteousness that can satisfy our Holy God could never be attained by a performance of fallen man, God Himself, in mercy, clothes the believer with His own righteousness. The believer receives the gift by a simple act of faith. Righteousness is strictly a gift received from God. Romans 5:17 clearly states: *"they which receive ABUNDANCE OF GRACE and the GIFT OF RIGHTEOUSNESS shall reign in life by one, Jesus Christ."* Moreover, the Scriptures declare: *"We are more than conquerors through Him who loved us"* (Rom.8:37). The very, very best we can produce in righteousness is as filthy rags in God's sight (Isaiah 64:6). Righteousness, therefore, is not a performance on our part. Righteousness is something only God can give His sinful creatures. Righteousness is not what we do; it is what we are, or are not. *"But of Him are ye IN CHRIST JESUS, who of God is made unto us wisdom, and RIGHTEOUSNESS and sanctification, and redemption"* (1Cor.1:30). That glorious revelation was given first to the carnal Corinthians, and applies to every blood bought child of God.

Millionaires ignorant of their great wealth

True accounts are told of millionaires caught digging in garbage pails to find scraps of food to keep them alive. They were totally ignorant of the millions of dollars gifted to them until someone hunted them down and informed them of their vast wealth. These true stories illustrate in an amazing way how the apostle Paul, led of the Spirit, handled the carnal Corinthian situation. The apostle informed them of the vast and inexhaustible wealth they were in possession of in Christ their Lord. The millionaires referred to in this story did not become less wealthy because of their conduct so out of keeping with their wealth. Neither were the carnal Corinthians *ever told they were less wealthy* because of their bad conduct that was so out of keeping with their wealth. Like the millionaires, they needed to be informed of the truth by an honest witness who knew of the inexhaustible resources and the wonderfully high position that was theirs in Christ Jesus their Lord. The knowledge of their incredible wealth brought about a repentance on the part of the millionaires. They immediately changed their lifestyle. When the Corinthians were made aware of their enormous wealth, and the goodness God poured out upon them, they also repented, which resulted in a changed lifestyle on their part

(2Cor.7:9). The original Greek word for repent is metanoeo, meaning 180 degree change of mind. We have an illustration of this fact in Matthew 21:28,29: *"But what think ye? A certain man had two sons; and he came to the first, and said, son, go work today in my vineyard. He answered and said, I will not; but afterward he repented, and went.'*

The righteousness a believer possesses is given by God's grace alone. It is THE RIGHTEOUSNESS OF GOD imputed by God the instant the believer receives Christ as Saviour. (1Cor.1:30; 2Cor.5:21). The most contemptible notion entertained by the believer is the notion that he is capable of a performance that needs to be added to the righteousness God has freely imparted to him. Think of what a terrible insult it is to the all inclusive, matchless, pure and altogether holy righteousness of God. What a terrible insult also to the work our blessed Saviour accomplished on the cruel Cross in order that He could righteously clothe us with Himself. *"Who shall not fear thee, O Lord and glorify thy name? For THOU ONLY ART HOLY: for all nations shall come and worship before thee"* (Rev.15:4).

William Law wrote the following great truths in his day. He lived in the early 1700's: *"'There is but one that is good, and that is God.' This was true when*

God had as yet created nothing. And this truth has not changed after He has created innumerable hosts of blessed and holy heavenly beings. Therefore, any goodness in the creature can be nothing but the one goodness of God manifesting a birth and discovery of itself as the created nature is fitted to receive it. No creature could produce of itself that which is good and blessed any more than it could create itself. 'The heavens', said David, 'declare the glory of God' and no creature, any more than the heavens, can declare any other glory. As well might it be said that the firmament shows forth its own handiwork, as that any man shows forth his own goodness.

"The Spirit of the triune God, breathed into Adam at his creation, was that alone which made him a holy creature in the image and likeness of God. A new birth of this Spirit of God in man is as necessary to make fallen man alive again unto God as it was to make Adam at first in the image and likeness of God. And a constant flow of this divine life by the Spirit is as necessary to man's continuance in his redeemed state as light and moisture are to the continued life of a plant. A religion that is not wholly built upon this supernatural ground, but which stands to any degree upon human powers, reasonings, and conclusions, has not so much as the shadow of truth in it. Such religion leaves man with mere empty

forms and images that can no more restore divine life to his soul than an idol of clay or wood could create another Adam.

"True Christianity is nothing but the continual dependence upon God through Christ for all life, light, and virtue, and the false religion of Satan is to seek that goodness from any other source. So the true child of God acknowledges that 'no man can receive anything except it be given him from above.' All goodness comes from God just as surely as all life comes from God. The highest angel has no more of his own that he can offer unto God than the poorest creature upon earth. Were an angel to imagine that the smallest degree of wisdom, goodness, or excellence came from or belonged to himself, his place in heaven would be lost as surely as Lucifer lost his. But songs of praise to their heavenly father are the angels' ravishing delight, because they never cease to acknowledge God as the source of all good in themselves and in the whole creation. This the one religion of heaven, and nothing else is the truth of religion upon earth." 1

The Saints of God at Corinth, carnal Corinthians (their conduct was atrocious), were emphatically informed at the outset of the letter that they were sanctified, justified and fellowshippers by God's calling (1Cor.1:2,9). We are informed in Romans

11:29, Amp: *"God's gifts and His call are irrevocable - He never withdraws them when once they are given, and He does not change His mind about those to whom He gives His grace or to whom He sends His call."* It should go without saying that what was true of the Corinthians is true of all believers for all time. Paul's Spirit-directed approach to the carnal Corinthians is in exact keeping with how an honest person (who knew of his wealth) would approach a multi-millionaire digging for sustenance in a garbage pail. He would immediately inform him of his enormous possessions, and I am sure he would advise him to claim his incredible wealth immediately and live in keeping with it. Too often, like the Corinthians, we are ignorant of God's illimitable resources that are always available for our constant enjoyment. Our lack of dependence on God results in poor conduct. However, we can thank God *"If we are faithless, He remains faithful; for He cannot deny Himself"* (2Tim. 2:13, NAS). The deadly "in-and-out-of-fellowship" notion attempts to destroy the marvelous truth found in that verse.

Jesus paid it all

I used to visit a government-subsidized home for the elderly. On one of my visits I observed something that made me quite sad. One of the workers in that home was coaxing one of the residents to go to the dining room where dinner was being served. I noticed that he was a well dressed man wearing what appeared to be a good quality brown suit. The dear man kept refusing to go, with the plea that he had no money to pay for his dinner. He probably did not have a nickel in his pocket, but he was totally unaware that everything to do with his complete welfare, including the dinner that was prepared for him, was already paid for to the full. Moreover, he was evidently unaware that his continued care was guaranteed by the Government of Canada for the rest of his life. How many of us are like that dear man, prone to look at our own spiritual resources, only to find they are always painfully inadequate. As a result we go on living in self-imposed poverty, never enjoying the inexhaustible resources of God that He has prepared and reserved for us. God has a great banquet hall, He has reserved a special place for every blood-bought believer, He has clothed us with His spotless righteousness, and dinner is now being served. Jesus said: *"Behold I stand at the door and knock: if any man hear my voice, and open the door, I will come in to him, and [dine] with him, and he with me"* (Rev.3:20). Our loving God Himself has provided everything we will ever need and enjoy, both for the present time and for all the ages of eternity. His great treasure-store contains good things that boggle our wildest imagination. Like the dear man in the rest home, we have no money. But God is coaxing us to come and dine on that heavenly fare. Jesus our loving Lord has paid the bill to the full. Moreover, He has made us heirs of God and joint heirs with Christ (Rom.8:17). Amazing grace!!

> *Amazing grace how sweet the sound that*
> *saved a wretch like me!*
> *I once was lost but now am found, was*
> *blind but now I see.*
>
> *'Twas grace that taught my heart to fear,*
> *and grace my fears relieved;*
> *How precious did that grace appear the*
> *hour I first believed.*
>
> *Through many dangers, toils and snares,*
> *I have already come;*
> *'Tis grace that brought me safe thus far,*
> *and grace will lead me home.*
>
> *When we've been there ten thousand*
> *years, bright shining as the sun,*
> *We've no less days to sing God's praise*
> *than when we've first begun.*

John Newton

God reckons the ungodly
believer righteous (Rom.4:5)

W.R.Newell elaborates on the great eternal truths referenced above. They need to be sounded from the housetops in order that believers who are now in bondage might be set free:

"If God announces the gift of righteousness apart from works, why do you keep mourning over your bad works, your failures? Do you not see that it is because you still have hopes in these works of yours that you are depressed and discouraged by their failures? If you truly saw and believed that God is reckoning righteous the UNGODLY who believe on Him, you would fairly hate your struggles to be 'better', for you would see that your dreams of good works have not at all commended you to God, and that your bad works do not at all hinder you from believing on Him - that justifieth the UNgodly! (Rom.4:5)

"Therefore, on seeing your failures, you should say, I am nothing but a failure, but God is dealing with me on another principle altogether than my works, good or bad, - a principle not involving my works, but based only on the work of Christ for me. I am anxious, indeed, to be pleasing to God and to be filled with His Spirit, but I am not at all justified, or accounted righteous, by these things. God, in

justifying me, acted wholly and only on Christ's [sacrifice] on my behalf. (Do not miss this great truth).

"Therefore, I have this double attitude: first, I know that Christ is in Heaven before God for me, and that I stand in the value before God of His finished work, that God sees me nowhere else but in this dead, buried and risen Christ, and that His favour is toward me in Christ, is limitless and eternal. (That is why the need to confess sins is foreign to every letter addressed specifically to believers in the New Testament.)

"Then, second, toward the work of the Holy Spirit in me, my attitude is a desire to be guided into the truth, to be obedient thereto, and to be chastened by God my Father if disobedient, to learn to pray in the Spirit, to walk by the Spirit, and to be filled with a love for the Scriptures and for the saints and for all men.

YET NONE OF THESE THINGS JUSTIFIES ME! I HAD JUSTIFICATION FROM GOD AS A SINNER, NOT AS A SAINT! My saintliness does not increase it, nor praise God, do my failures decrease it!" 2   (Note: Comments in brackets are mine.)

Error substituted for liberating truth

I hope you have not missed the glaring contrast

between the teaching of the inspired apostle (Paul) and the teaching that so sadly abounds today. He never taught that a believer can be **in and out of fellowship. Confession of sin, asking for forgiveness, is totally foreign and opposite to what he was led of God to write.** When addressing the carnal Corinthians he rather reinforced the great truth of their eternal unity with our loving and great God. When born-again believers sin today in a similar manner to the Corinthians, they are taught the opposite. They are taught that their fellowship with God is broken and cannot be restored until they confess their sins to God. The apostle Paul, however, could reinforce the great truth of the eternal and changeless standing and state (so called) of the carnal Corinthians because it is a work of God in its entirety. God can righteously clothe all who believe because of the finished work on the Cross, the ongoing cleansing of the precious blood, and the work of intercession continually being undertaken on their behalf. The revelation of these great truths to the believer is the only remedy that will effect deliverance from sin and worldliness.

God dealt with the Corinthians on the amazing principle revealed to us in Romans 2:4: *"The goodness of God leadeth [thee] to repentance".* The apostle's revelation of God's great goodness quickly moved the carnal Corinthians to a positive repentance. They learned the truth that their loving God was not standing over them with a club, neither did He sever them from fellowship because of their horrible conduct. He was rather living within them, closer to them than the limbs of their own bodies. God's Word to the carnal Corinthians is forever settled in heaven, and applies to every believer without exception: *"He that is joined unto the Lord is ONE spirit"* and *"What? Know ye not that your body is the temple of the Holy Spirit which is in you, which ye have of God, and ye are not your own? For ye are bought with a price: therefore glorify God in your body, and in your spirit, which are God's"* (1Cor.6:17,19,20). That amazing truth applies to every believer, every day of his life on earth, and on and on into eternity. To undo that glorious relationship, the work of our loving Saviour on the Cross would have to be undone.

Fellowship strictly a calling of God

The Spirit of God, through Paul, never taught the Corinthians or any other group of believers that they could lose fellowship with God, even though they were living a life of carnality. **Where do we get the authority to teach that carnal believers are out of fellowship with God?** Certainly not from the Word of God. If believers could get out of fellowship by bad conduct and had to confess their sins in order to be restored to fellowship, the letters to the Corinthians and to the Galatians would repeatedly give that instruction. But such instruction is **foreign** to the inspired epistles of God's appointed apostle Paul who was given the rounded-out truth of the gospel. Re-read Galatians 1:8,9; its consequences are most serious indeed. We **would be wise** to **test** what we have been taught by placing ourselves in the apostle's shoes, and confronting the carnal Corinthians as he did. Our reaction can quickly be tested by the Word of God. Suppose we were fully informed, as the apostle was, that the Corinthians were sinning before God. How would we greet them? If we are teaching truth, our answer will correspond with the words given them by the Spirit-directed apostle. *"I thank my God always on your behalf, for the grace of God which is given you by Jesus Christ; that in everything ye are enriched by Him, in all utterance, and in all knowledge; even as the testimony of Christ was confirmed in you: so that ye come behind in no gift; waiting for the coming of our Lord Jesus Christ: who also shall confirm you unto the end, that ye may be blameless in the day of our Lord Jesus Christ. God is faithful, by whom YE WERE CALLED UNTO THE FELLOWSHIP OF HIS SON JESUS CHRIST OUR LORD"* (1Cor.1:4-9).

What an amazing word of truth to the carnal Corinthians. How would we fare on that one? Would we have difficulty telling them they were still in fellowship, despite their carnality (v.9)? Would we inform them that Christ is their only righteousness? (1:30) What would we teach them in view of the envyings, strife, and divisions among them? (3:3). Would we tell them they were out of fellowship with God and needed to confess their sins asking God for forgiveness? Or would we inform them as did the Spirit-led apostle, *"ye are God's [cultivated field], ye are God's building?* (1Cor.3:9). *"Therefore let no man glory in men. For ALL THINGS ARE YOUR'S; whether Paul, or Apollos, or Cephas, or the world, or life or death, or things present, or things to come; all are your's; and ye are Christ's; and Christ is God's"* (1Cor.3:21-23). Does that sound as though they were out of fellowship with God? Did you pass the test thus far? You know as well as I do that if we are true to present day teaching, respecting the so-called necessity to confess every sin in order to be forgiven, we could never reinforce to the carnal Corinthians the great truths given them by the Spirit-directed apostle.

It is very, very obvious that believers' confession of sin to God has been added to the pure gospel that Paul was given to preach. He was directed by the Spirit of God to declare in positive language that he was *"pure from the blood of ALL men. For I have not shunned to declare unto you ALL the counsel of God"* (Acts 20:27). Furthermore, he was directed by God to sound a frightening warning (Gal.1:8,9) to all who dare add anything to the rounded-out gospel he miraculously received from Jesus the Lord.

We will be wise if we continue through the Corinthian letters, to see if our thinking and teaching corresponds to that of the apostle. If not, we may need to **renounce** the error we are entertaining. Placing ourselves in the shoes of the chosen apostle and testing our reaction to the conduct of the Corinthian church is the greatest test to determine whether or not we are proclaiming God's truth. If our reaction to the atrocious conduct of the Corinthians is any different to that of the Spirit-directed apostle, we know that we have swallowed dangerous heresy somewhere along the way. That heresy must be repented of and flushed out by the liberating truth of the Word of God. Thank God for His truth which alone can set the captive free. The never changing truth of God will be manifest when we stand before Him, and on and on throughout the eternal ages.

CHAPTER 10

A guilt complex only God's revealed truth can remove

There is a very deep guilt complex entrenched within the human conscience as a result of the fall. That is why the error of continual introspection and confession of sin and asking for forgiveness is so acceptable to many believers. It gives us a great deal of satisfaction to be doing something, rather than just thanking God by faith that it is already done. Peter could never be hoodwinked with that error if he sat under our teaching today. Our blessed Lord showed him plainly that his sins were already taken care of long before he ever committed the acts (Luke 22:32). Adam and Eve demonstrated that guilt complex immediately after the fall when they began to take fig leaves to cover themselves. When God came to rescue them they ran for the trees (Gen.3).The covering they had provided by their own works was no protection from their guilt and shame. It did not satisfy them when God came on the scene, and it certainly never satisfied God.

Confession of sin to God, however, is for the one who has never repented. It is really just another type of **self effort** on the part of one whom God has already clothed with His own righteousness. If we refuse to fully accept the FINALITY OF THE

WORK DONE ON THE CROSS on our behalf, we will want to go on confessing our sins and asking for forgiveness. Self effort does not die easily. Ongoing confession of sin to God provides at least some satisfactory ground for fleshly performance.

Believing is the only work God requires of man

A notable example of the deeply entrenched notion that we can perform for God was demonstrated by those who came to Jesus and asked Him, *"what must we do to work the works of God?"* They were abysmally ignorant of the fact that man is totally incapable of doing anything for God. Our Lord's reply should also silence forever the false notion that God needs a performance (other than simply believing) on the part of any man. His reply will ring down through the ages of eternity. Do not miss the finality of it: *"This is the work of God, that ye believe on [rely on, trust in] Him whom He has sent"* (John 6:28,29). That great truth is in perfect harmony with the entire canon of Scripture with respect to the believers' walk with God.

One simple but most profound verse spells out the divine principle of the Christian walk very, very clearly. It applies to every believer without exception: *"As ye have therefore received Christ Jesus the Lord, so walk ye in Him"* (Col.2:6). This wonderful command is one of the most critical commands pertaining to the Christian walk found in the New Testament. When our Saviour awakened us from our death state in trespasses and sins, our attitude had to be one of total surrender. We had no ability whatsoever to save ourselves. He had to do 100% of the saving. Now that He has saved us, we are to maintain the same attitude of total dependence that we adopted when we were saved. Our God never created us with the capacity to do anything on our own. Our Lord and Saviour spoke with a divine finality when He declared: *"Without Me you can do nothing"* (John 15:5). Our own plans and schemes count for nothing in the eternal economy of God. When we wholeheartedly accept the truth that we can do nothing by ourselves, we discover the first secret of the Christian walk. As we maintain a life of total dependance on Him, He does 100% of the work He wants done through our yielded members. There is only one who can live the Christian life and that one is Christ Himself, because He **IS** the Christian life. That great truth is stated very clearly in the Word of God: *"When Christ, who IS our life, shall appear, then shall ye also appear with Him in glory"* (Col.3:4).

God's covering alone adequate

When God sacrificed innocent animals to provide Adam and Eve with a covering, they knew ever after that they were totally acceptable in His presence (Gen.3:21). The covering He provided for them had nothing whatsoever to do with any effort on their part. Having RECEIVED that initial covering provided by God, whether they did better or worse in the succeeding years of their lives, God's covering remained. When they subsequently sinned they could stroke God's covering and *THANK HIM* that it remained, for they knew that it was provided by the blood shedding and death of an innocent one. I am sure they very well knew that God does not demand payment twice. Therefore, it was a constant reminder to them that a covering of **God's** provision alone made them acceptable in His sight. Since His covering was sufficient to make them acceptable after the **terrible sin of the initial fall,** they could rest assured that it was abundantly adequate to maintain that acceptance in the succeeding years of their lives on earth.

The magnitude of Adam's sin at the initial fall could **NEVER** be repeated. The consequences of it are **so great** and **so terrible** that no human creature on earth could ever grasp it. Nevertheless, our great loving God went forth to seek out Adam and Eve.

He forgave them freely and clothed them with a covering that made them fit once again to stand in His Holy presence. When we consider that God fully knew beforehand that Adam's sin would pollute **every generation for thousands of years to come,** we cannot miss the magnitude of His glorious grace and His infinite love. That love and that grace is extended to us all. The covering that was provided Adam and Eve is but a shadow or type of our Lord Jesus Christ who died in our stead, **took away** our sins and clothed us with the gift of His righteousness which **alone** fits us to stand faultless before His throne both now and forevermore. That great demonstration of God's mercy and grace at the outset of man's dreadful fall should speak volumes to us for ever.

C.H. MacIntosh comments on the Genesis account. *"'Unto Adam, also, and to his wife, did the Lord God make coats of skins, and clothed them.' We have here, in figure, the great doctrine of divine righteousness set forth. The robe which God provided was an effectual covering, because He provided it; just as the apron was an ineffectual covering, because man had provided it. Moreover, God's coat was founded upon blood-shedding; Adam's apron was not. So also now, God's righteousness is set forth in the Cross; man's righteousness is set forth in the works - the sin stained works - of his own hands. When Adam stood clothed in the coat of skin he could not say he was naked, nor had he any occasion to hide himself. The sinner may feel perfectly at rest when, by faith, he knows that God has clothed him; but to feel at rest till then, can only be the result of presumption or ignorance. To know that the dress I wear, and in which I appear before God, is of His own providing, must set my heart at perfect rest. There can be no true, permanent rest in aught else".* 1

Believers confession nullifies positive truth

When we start with the premise that 1John 1:9 is instruction for the born-again Christian to confess his sins in order to be forgiven by God, we in effect destroy the great positive truths revealed by the Holy Spirit through the gospel writers that we are already totally forgiven. These truths are:

1. Justified - ***"God justifies the UNgodly"*** (Rom.4:5).

2. Sealed - ***"sealed with that Holy Spirit of promise"*** (Eph.1:13).

3. Perfected - ***"He has perfected forever them that are sanctified"*** (Heb.10:14).

4. Clothed with the righteousness of Christ - ***"But***

of Him are ye in Christ Jesus, who of God is made unto us wisdom, and righteousness, and sanctification, and redemption" (1Cor.1:30).

5. Raised to a new life - He has *"raised us up together, and made us sit together in heavenly places in Christ Jesus"* (Eph.2:6).

6. Forgiven forever - *"Be it known unto you therefore, men and brethren, that through this man is preached unto you the FORGIVENESS OF SINS: and by Him all that believe are JUSTIFIED FROM ALL THINGS, from which ye could not be justified by the law of Moses"* (Acts 13:38,39). *"In whom we have redemption through His blood, THE FORGIVENESS OF SINS, according to the riches of His grace"* (Eph.1:7). *"Be ye kind one to another, tenderhearted, forgiving one another, even as God for Christ's sake HATH FORGIVEN YOU"* (Eph.4:32). *"Who hath delivered us from the power of darkness, and hath translated us into the kingdom of His dear son: in whom we have redemption through His blood, even THE FORGIVENESS OF SINS"* (Col.1:13,14). *"And you, being dead in your sins and the uncircumcision of your flesh, hath He [made alive] together with Him, HAVING FORGIVEN YOU ALL TRESPASSES"*

(Col.2:13). *"Forbearing one another, and forgiving one another, if any man have a quarrel against any: even as CHRIST FORGAVE YOU, so also do ye"* (Col.3:13). *"I write unto you, little children, because YOUR SINS ARE FORGIVEN YOU for His name's sake"* (1John 2:12).

In view of the above great and precious New Covenant promises, is it any wonder that the chosen apostles of God never once taught believers to confess their sins asking for forgiveness? To do so would contradict every great promise referred to above.

Since our great God knows the future as well as He knows the past, we can rest assured that *all* of our sins past, present and future (for all our sins were future when our Saviour died) are totally forgiven. What then can we do? Rejoice and abound in thanksgiving (Col.2:7) giving honour *"unto Him that loved us, and washed us from our sins by His own blood"* (Rev.1:5). *"To Him be glory both now and forever. Amen"* (2Peter 3:18).

As we close this study on confession of sin in respect to the believer it is our hope that many eyes may be opened to see that the traditions of men, as in Jesus' day, (Mark7:13) have made the Word of God of no effect in many cases. May our thoughts and our teaching bow in obedience to the Word of God. May the words of the chosen apostle and teacher of the Gentiles arrest us as never before: *"But though we, or an Angel from heaven, preach any other gospel unto you than that which we have preached unto you, let him be accursed. As we said before, so say I now again, if any man preach any other gospel unto you than that ye have received, let him be accursed"* (Gal.1:8,9). The same apostle records several confrontations with sinning saints, but never once did he ever preach confession of sin to God on the part of believers. **Do you or I dare add to what he taught?**

We should seriously consider seven critical things respecting the miraculous calling and commission of the apostle Paul, the chosen teacher of the Gentiles.

1. He received the complete and rounded-out gospel directly from our glorious Lord (Gal.1:12).

2. He compared what he had received from the Lord with the chief apostles, Peter, James and John. He was directed by the Spirit to record that they added nothing to what he had already received (Gal 2:6).

3. He declared by the Spirit: *"I am pure from the blood of all men. For I have not shunned to*

declare unto you the whole counsel of God" (Acts 20:26,27). Therefore, we can say with positive assurance that believers' confession, asking God's forgiveness, is not part of the Counsel of God. The Spirit-breathed Scriptures record his counsel to several sinning saints but he never spoke a single word to them respecting the supposed need to confess to God the sins they had committed.

4. He was selected by God to write marvelous revelations and new covenant instructions which the Spirit wanted to reveal to the Churches.

5. He was chosen of God to write the greater part of the New Testament.

6. He was instructed of God to sound a frightening warning to anyone who will dare add to the rounded-out truth that was given to him by our Lord (Gal.1:8,9).

7. We may search and research the entire canon of Scripture that was supernaturally given to Paul, but we will never find a single reference where he taught believers to confess their sins to God. Furthermore, the widespread teaching that a believer can lose fellowship with God because of misconduct is utterly foreign to the Spirit inspired truth of Scripture. The greatest revelations regarding the believers eternal unity

with God are found in contexts where carnal Corinthian believers were sinning like the heathen around them.

God forbid that the writer of this book, or those who have read it, ever be guilty of adding to the rounded-out truth taught by Paul to God's choice people. When we quit confessing our sins that our Saviour bare *"in His own body on the tree"* (1Pet.2:24) we are then, and only then, ready to obey our dear Lord's command. *"Reckon ye also yourselves to be DEAD indeed unto sin, but ALIVE unto God through Jesus Christ our Lord"* (Rom.6:11).

Let us acknowledge His truth right now and *"stand fast in the liberty wherewith Christ hath made us free, and be not again entangled in the yoke of bondage"* (Gal.5:1). Our Sodom days are over - forever. We are told not to look back by morbid introspection. Our release is complete and final. Our blessed Saviour has paid our debt to the full. We have been translated (not into another location on earth as Lot was) but *"from the power of darkness...into the kingdom of His dear son: in whom we have redemption through His blood even the forgiveness of sins"* (Col.1:13).

We are not to be *"conformed to this world: but be ye transformed by the renewing of your mind"*

(Rom.12:2). When we received Christ a death by crucifiction with Him occurred (Gal.2:20). Our God who lives in the eternally present, placed us in Christ and saw us die with Him on the cursed tree. His word declares *"ye are dead, and your life is hid with Christ in God. When Christ, who is our life, shall appear, then shall ye also appear with Him in glory"* (Col.3:3,4). Since we were raised with Christ to live a resurrection life (Col.3:1) our focus ought to have changed for ever. Our new habitation is in the heavenlies where *"He hath raised us up together, and made us sit together in heavenly places in Christ Jesus"* (Eph.2:6). We are a new creation in Christ, old things are passed away; *"behold all things are become new"* (2Cor.5:17). We must always keep in mind that God has declared *"ye are all the children of light and the children of the day: we are not of the night, nor of darkness"* (1Thes.5:5).

Dear believer in Jesus Christ our Saviour, it is our great desire that you have eternally profited from this particular research in the great Word of God. If you have been a good Berean and have conducted your own research, you will have discovered for yourself that our loving God **NEVER** commanded His New Covenant people to keep on confessing their sins to Him. Such a command is nowhere to be found in His rounded-out direction to His beloved

Church. Ongoing confession was mandatory for those who were under the Old Covenant. They had to offer a sacrifice every time confession was made (Lev 5:5-19). The offering had to take the offerer's place in death. Every sacrificial death was an execution of the sentence of the law under the Old Covenant.

Oh, what a glorious contrast to live under the New Covenant. *"Christ, our passover, is sacrificed for us"* (1Cor.5:7). Our loving Saviour declared: *"This is my blood of the* **NEW** *[Covenant], which is shed for many for the [forgiveness] of sins"* (Matt.26:28). *"through the Eternal Spirit [He] offered Himself without spot to God* (Heb.9:14) for the sole purpose of *"[bearing] our sins in His own body on the tree"* (1Peter 2:24). *"He is able [therefore] to save them to the uttermost that come unto God by Him, seeing He ever liveth to make intercession for them"* (Heb.7:25). Confession of sin with animal offerings had to be repeated over and over again. But now *"by one offering He hath perfected forever them that are sanctified"* (Heb.10:14). If we refuse to believe that the work of Jesus Christ our Lord was sufficient to perfect us forever, we will keep on running back as the Hebrews did under the Old Covenant, begging God to forgive us.

If we have been deeply entrenched in the common notion that we must continually confess our sins to God asking for repeated forgiveness (a command nowhere to be found in the New Testament) we will find it very difficult to flush it out of our minds. The very best way to overcome that notion is to obey God and put into continual practice the blessed commands that are commands indeed. *"Rejoice in the Lord always, and again I say rejoice"* (Phil.4:4). *"Rejoice evermore"* (1Thes.5:16). *"By him therefore let us offer the sacrifice of praise continually, the fruit of our lips, giving thanks to His name"* (Heb.13:15). The time we spend confessing sins that He put away by the sacrifice of Himself, robs us of time we ought to be spending in heartfelt praise and thanksgiving to Him who *"bore our sins in His own body on the tree"* (1Peter 2:24). Moreover, He *"saves them to the UTTERMOST that come unto God by him, seeing He ever liveth to make intercession for them"* (Heb.7:25). Let us cease trying to usurp his office.

When we wholeheartedly accept God's glorious truth that we are forgiven forever the over-flowing grace of God floods into our hearts enabling us to fulfill every command with abounding joy. *"Grace and peace be yours in abundance through the knowledge of God and of Jesus our Lord. His divine power has given us everything we need for life and godliness"* (2Pet.1:2,3NIV).

If perchance you have read this book and have never received Jesus Christ as your Saviour and Lord, 1John 1:9 is a promise written to you. *"If [you] confess [your] sins, he is faithful and just to forgive [you your] sins.* (The tense used in the original indicates once and forever) *and [will] cleanse you from all unrighteousness."* The instant you have confessed your sins, as the publican did of old, you will go down to your house justified (Luke 18:13,14). God always makes good His promises and *"whatsoever God doeth, it shall be forever; nothing can be put to it, nor any thing taken from it"* (Ecc.3:14). Do not procrastinate. Do it now and you will hear His command: *"Rejoice evermore."* When He forgives you, you are forgiven forever.

CHAPTER NOTES

Prologue

1 J. Vernon McGee, "1 John" (Pasadena Ca, 1979), p. 33

2 The International Standard Bible Encyclopedia, (Grand Rapids: Eerdmans, 1949), Vol.11 p.1243.

Chapter 1

1 Vines Complete Expository Dictionary, (Nashville: Thomas Nelson 1979), p. 33

2 J.Sidlow Baxter, "A new call to holiness" (Grand Rapids: Zondervan, 1985), p. 120

Chapter 2

1Hal Lindsey, "Amazing Grace" (Western Front: Ltd, 1995), pp. 162-164

Chapter 5

1 Encyclopedia Britannica (Chicago 1958), Vol. 10 p. 452

2 E. Pagels, "The Gnostic Gospels" (New York Vintage Books, 1979), p. 12

3 E. Pagels, "The Gnostic Gospels" (New York Vintage Books, 1979), p. 11

4 J. Vernon McGee, "1 John" (Pasadena, Ca. 1979), p. 19

5 The International Standard Bible Ency. (Grand Rapids: Eerdmans, 1949), Vol.3 p. 1712.

Chapter 6

1 K.S. Wuest, "Word studies in Romans" (Grand Rapids: Eerdmans, 1973), p. 146

Chapter 7

1 W. R. Newell, "Romans Verse by Verse" (Chicago: Moody Press, 1938), pp. 224-226.

2 Ibid. pp. 215-216.

3 K. S. Wuest "Studies in the Vocabulary of the Greek New Testament" (Grand Rapids: Eerdmans, 1973), p. 37.

4 H. A. Ironsides, "Galatians & Ephesians" (New York: Loizeaux Brothers Inc. 1983), pp. 71-72

Chapter 8

1 Steve McVey, "Grace Walk" (Harvest House 1996)

Chapter 9

1 William Law, "The Power of the Spirit," edited by Dave Hunt (Fort Wash.: Christian Literature Crusade 1971), pp. 15-16.

2 W. R. Newell, "Romans Verse by Verse" (Chicago: Moody Press 1938), p. 129

Chapter 10

1 C. H. MacIntosh, "Notes on Genesis" (New York: Loizeaux Brothers Inc., 1956), pp 54-55.

APPENDIX

Here are some of the comments I have received (some from personal contact, stated as near as I can recall, and quotes directly from letters received) from those who have read this manuscript before it was finally completed. These testimonies speak for themselves and reveal the power of God to release and set the captive free in every area where error binds the children of God.

1. A missionary who spent several years on the foreign field writes about her wonderful release:*"What an amazing doctrine God has revealed. I have never experienced such liberation nor felt so eternally secure as I did after reading this Manuscript. Imagine what this would do for someone just delivered from Catholicism. May God use this mightily for His glory."* E. K.

2. From a man who has been a faithful worker in the church for 25 years: *"I have been restored to my first love of my Saviour after reading your manuscript."* L.T.

3. A lengthy telephone call from a pastor: *"I have been a Christian for 30 years. I have preached the eternal security of the believer as it is revealed in the Word of God, for several years, but I was never sure of my own security until I*

saw that the Word of God does not teach that a believer needs to confess his sins to God, asking for forgiveness on a continual basis. Please send me anything else that you have written." B.F.

4. An old saint of God who loves and has studied the Word of God for many years had this response: *"I thank you for the manuscript sent from Hector. I cannot tell you how much this light means to me. It surely is light, as I realize how many years of harassment Satan has laid upon me. I cannot deny the fact* (that confession of sins to God is *NOT* directed to the believer) *as all scripture proves otherwise".* M.L. (After considering the above response, the question occurred to me: Could anyone establish by a Court decision that ongoing confession of sin asking for forgiveness is necessary for the believer under the New Covenant? It is obvious that no one could ever get a Court hearing because there is no evidence in the Bible to support it. Court officials would require several clear references from the lips of our risen Saviour, and from Paul the chosen apostle and teacher to the gentiles who addressed the several churches. Upon discovering that neither the risen Saviour nor the apostle ever taught believers ongoing confession of their sins for forgiveness, they would throw out the case for

lack of evidence. It would be a waste of Court time. That fact requires very serious consideration as our final accounting will be based on the eternal Word of God which He has given to us. The notions of men will go up in smoke, offering no shelter for those who have accepted them).

5. From an ex-preacher written personally by himself: *"Since embracing this "new" truth of my spontaneous and immediate forgiveness, I am now free to enjoy unbroken fellowship with my Saviour. e.g. late one evening through an argument with my sister, I sinned by wrong attitude, cutting words, and no apology. Formerly I would have wasted the intervening time believing I was "out of fellowship" with the Lord. Instead He gave me a day brimming with His acceptance, guidance and fellowship. That evening I did "confess my faults" to my sister. But that one day was an eye-opening experience, proving to me that His sweet unbroken fellowship would never again have to rest on my conduct, but on His! "If any man sin, we have an Advocate with the Father, Jesus Christ the righteous" 1John 2:1."* P.B. (One wonders how many of God's dear people have swallowed the falsehood that fellowship with our dear Lord can be severed because of some

fault or failure in our walk. The Bema seat alone will reveal the loss suffered and the precious hours of fellowship forfeited as a result of that erroneous teaching. The detailed account of Peter's grievous sin and our Lord's loving and changeless attitude toward him shows how far out our notions can be.)

6. A couple who study and love the Word of God were given a copy of this manuscript and wrote: *"After years of Bible study...Hal and I had long ago reached the understanding that confession of sins by the believer was not actually in the Word. I was excited to see that Pastor MacLeod interprets 1John 1:9 like I do. But it is especially gratifying to see the truth proclaimed so thoroughly and in such positive and forceful language. I wish every pastor, teacher, and evangelist in the world could read this. I appreciate so much your making this available. I believe it will help me encourage others, as I am encouraged, to enjoy the freedom and prosperity that is mine in Christ Jesus."* L.S.

From a lady who received an earlier manuscript.and some of my messages on cassettes. She states in her letter: *"I have made copies* (of the tapes, and the manuscript) *for pastors and lay people...I can't thank the Lord enough for working in you and through you. I can't explain the joy the Lord has given my husband, myself and my sister. I am just like a child, so free. I cannot explain the joy of the heavenly Father's love for me. My childhood has been restored, and I just can't wait to share the gospel with everyone".* C. C.

God's great message of positive truth to all believers can never be annulled, it will ring down through the eternal ages. "These things have I written unto you that believe on the name of the Son of God; that you may KNOW that you HAVE eternal life" (1John 5:13). "I write unto you, little children, because YOUR SINS ARE FORGIVEN YOU for HIS name's sake." (1John 2:12). May we never be guilty of doubting God's great Word for a single moment, and may His name alone ever be praised.